INVASION OF THE PLUSH MONSTERS!

INVASION OF THE PLUSH MONSTERS!

Wickedly Weird Creatures You Just Gotta Sew

Veronika Alice Gunter

Illustrations by John Murphy

LARK BOOKS

A Division of Sterling Publishing Co., Inc.
New York / London

Library of Congress Cataloging-in-Publication Data

Gunter, Veronika Alice.
  Invasion of the plush monsters : wickedly weird creatures you just gotta
sew / Veronika Alice Gunter.
      p. cm.
  Includes index.
  ISBN-13: 978-1-57990-943-7 (hc-plc with jacket : alk. paper)
  ISBN-10: 1-57990-943-4 (hc-plc with jacket : alk. paper)
  1. Soft toy making. I. Title.
  TT174.3.G86 2008
  745.592'4--dc22

                                            2007040388

10 9 8 7 6 5 4 3 2 1

First Edition

Published by Lark Books, A Division of
Sterling Publishing Co., Inc.
387 Park Avenue South, New York, NY 10016

© 2008 Text, illustrations, and photography, Lark Books

Distributed in Canada by Sterling Publishing,
c/o Canadian Manda Group, 165 Dufferin Street
Toronto, Ontario, Canada M6K 3H6

Distributed in the United Kingdom by GMC Distribution Services,
Castle Place, 166 High Street, Lewes, East Sussex, England BN7 1XU

Distributed in Australia by Capricorn Link (Australia) Pty Ltd.,
P.O. Box 704, Windsor, NSW 2756 Australia

The written instructions, photographs, designs, patterns, and projects in this volume are intended for
the personal use of the reader and may be reproduced for that purpose only. Any other use, especially
commercial use, is forbidden under law without written permission of the copyright holder.

Every effort has been made to ensure that all the information in this book is accurate. However, due to
differing conditions, tools, and individual skills, the publisher cannot be responsible for any injuries, losses,
and other damages that may result from the use of the information in this book.

If you have questions or comments about this book, please contact:
Lark Books
67 Broadway
Asheville, NC 28801
828-253-0467

Manufactured in China

ISBN 13: 978-1-57990-943-7
ISBN 10: 1-57990-943-4

For information about custom editions, special sales, premium and corporate purchases, please contact
Sterling Special Sales Department at 800-805-5489 or specialsales@sterlingpub.com.

Art Director: Robin Gregory
Photographer: Steve Mann
Cover Designer: Celia Naranjo
Art Assistant: Bradley Norris
Editorial Assistant: Rose McLarney

Acknowledgments

Toy designers John Murphy, Jenny
Harada, and Ian Dennis channeled the
spirits of these kooky creatures and made
them real. Thank you!

CONTENTS

They've Landed!

At first, the government and media tried to convince the people that nothing unusual was happening. Citizens were told to reject reports that the Hubble Space Telescope had photographed fuzzy aliens floating in nearby galaxies. Public service announcements directed everyone to stop spreading stories of chubby window-peeping creatures with button-like eyes. No one knew what to believe.

Then reports of sightings multiplied—exponentially. Could 300,000 drivers be wrong about a zipper-mouth critter taking a bite out of an overpass? Would the authorities persuade the people to believe their version of events, or would the people trust their own eyes?

The official message hasn't changed, but the truth is out.

They're beastly. They're bizarre. Though some call them monsters, they'd never cause harm—intentionally. And from the looks of things, these plush creatures are on the verge of taking over the Earth.

So, if you can't beat 'em, join 'em.

We've studied these strange invaders. We've created patterns and instructions so you can make replicas of them for yourself. Some even help you carry your books, gadgets, and more—just like in the stories you've heard. Construct these creatures from fabric, stuffing, and thread using sewing needles. Simple stuff!

Please note that the publisher is hereby relieved of all responsibility for the actions of any plush creatures you create.

—Veronika Alice Gunter

Fashioning Freaky Friends

This section will tell you all you need to know about the materials, tools, and skills you need to create the creepy and cute creatures invading the pages of this book. It also includes detailed **instructions**, **patterns**, and **diagrams** for making your first plush monster, Lyle the Horned Alien (pages 16-20). You don't need any **sewing** experience, but a little imagination will help you make your critters unique. (Words in boldface are in the glossary on page 94.)

Basic Beastie Kit

Each set of instructions refers to the Basic Beastie Kit. Collect the small items and store them in a basket or bag. Additional materials or tools needed for a particular critter will be listed in its What You Need list.

What You Need

- Photocopier, a pencil, and several sheets of letter-sized (8.5 x 11-inch [21.6 x 27.9 cm]) paper (to copy, or trace, and transfer patterns)
- Letter-sized card stock or poster board (to transfer patterns onto and create templates)
- Tape (to attach the patterns to the card stock or poster board)

- **Fabric pen** with permanent ink, or a fabric pencil, or fabric chalk (to make marks on fabric) **A**
- Sharpened pencil (to do math or make light marks on fabric)
- Measuring tape (to, um, measure) **B**
- **Craft scissors** (Use for paper, card stock, and thread.) **C**
- **Fabric scissors** (Use only for fabric.) **D**
- **Straight pins** (a whole pack of long pins with big, round, plastic or glass heads, to secure fabric in place before sewing) **E**
- Thimble (Wear it on the index finger of your nondominant hand while you hand sew, if you want to avoid stabbing yourself.)
- Polyester thread (One spool, any color. See page 9 for more about thread.)
- Upholstery thread (One spool, any color. See page 9 for more about thread.)
- Variety pack of general hand-sewing **needles** (Make sure you have general sewing, embroidery, and straw needles.) **F**
- Sewing machine (Optional but recommended for a few projects.)

A

B

C **D**

E

F

G

- Two packs of sewing-machine needles with universal needles (Get these if you're using a sewing machine. These needles break easily; that's why you need two packs.)

- Grade-two polyester fiber stuffing (Most projects require less than half a bag. See page 10 for more about stuffing.)

- Unsharpened pencil, wooden spoon, or dowel (to push stuffing inside a monster)

- Capped pen with a rounded point or **turning tool** (to get into corners for turning out ears and other odd shapes)

- **Seam ripper** (Optional. This tool can undo stitches, if you don't like how they look and want to try again.) **G**

Monster-Making Materials

You Need Fabric

These creatures are all made from soft, huggable materials. You'll see a lot of shaggy **polyester** (also called **faux fur**), fluffy **fleece**, and thick **felt**. Sometimes a thin **cotton** or polyester fabric is used for **lining** or **appendages** (legs, arms, ears, horns, etc.). Occasionally you'll use recycled clothing, such as neckties or a **felted** sweater. The project instructions tell you what kind of **fabric** to use for each creature. Buy what you need in fabric stores, thrift shops, or at yard sales. It might be a good idea to keep your plans for these fabrics to yourself. Some people are afraid of monsters, even friendly plush ones.

Threads That Bind

Sew your monsters together with polyester **thread**. But don't buy cheap thread. It's a sad day when your beastie bursts its **seams**, and that should only happen after years of fun together. So, buy good, moderately priced polyester thread instead. It's strong, yet light and thin enough to easily pass through fabric.

Use polyester **upholstery** thread for attaching buttons. It's smooth enough for sewing but still very sturdy. If you find upholstery thread easy to use, go ahead and use it for all the hand-sewing you do. Your **stitches** can be pulled tighter and your creatures will hold together longer. (You'll read more about stitches in Sewing Techniques & Terms on pages 11-15.)

Sinister, Hypnotic, or Just Plain Silly Eyes

Eyes go a long way toward creating personality on a face. These monsters have lots of personality—and as many as four eyes each. (You might even want to give your creations a few more.) The project instructions tell you what kind of eyes to use & how to attach them. You'll sew on **buttons** (read Sewing on Button Eyes on page 14), insert & snap on **child-safe doll eyes** or **cat eyes** (see Attaching the Child-Safe Eyes on pages 17-18), or use a **hot-glue gun** and **hot glue** to attach **googly eyes**. (Follow the hot-glue gun manufacturer's directions for use.) Buy these tools and materials at craft or fabric stores.

FLEECE

FAUX FUR

FELT

Inside Every Monster Is...Stuffing

Most of these creatures are squeezable because they're full of grade-two polyester fiber **stuffing**. It's inexpensive, a recycled product, and easy to wash and dry. (That means your monster keeps its shape even after a trip through the dryer.) So, use it! If you or the person you are making a critter for has allergies, however, use grade-one polyester stuffing. It's non-allergenic. **Batting** is another type of stuffing material. Each project's What You Need list will tell you what you need to fill out that creature. Buy the materials at craft or fabric stores. (You'll read about stuffing techniques on page 15.)

Patterns & Templates for Terrific & Terrible Plushies

Helpful, Friendly Patterns

A pattern is a guide for making something. Each monster-making project in this book includes patterns for different parts of that creature. The patterns have information you need to create a plush critter in the size and shape of a harmless companion. You certainly wouldn't want to make these monsters life size. Just look at Xipp It on page 50 to see what could happen.

What Patterns Tell You

- Names and letters to identify each part (head, A; body, B; etc.)
- How many pieces you'll cut of each pattern (1, 2, etc.)

- What color and type of fabric to use with each pattern piece (green fleece, red felt, etc.)
- Size that the pattern needs to be (If the pattern needs to be enlarged [enlarge 100 percent, etc.], there will be a note telling you to do that. Use a photocopier.)
- **Cut lines**, which are solid lines on the outside edges of each pattern
- **Seam allowance lines**, which are dotted lines ¼ to ⅜ inch (6 to 9.5 mm) inside the cut line on each pattern
- If a pattern has no seam allowance, you can expect that you'll **appliqué** the shape to another piece of fabric. (Read more about this technique in Appliqué on page 13.)
- Diagrams, if necessary, to show you where to place appliqués or how to align or arrange the pieces of the plush creature

Patterns and Diagrams

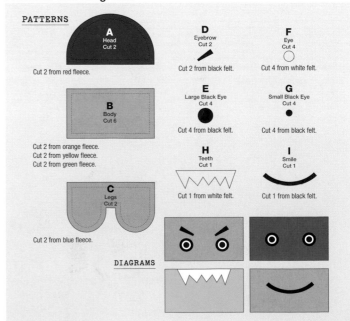

About Those Templates

You'll use the patterns to create **templates**. A template is a pattern cut from sturdy material such as card stock (a very thick paper). (See Making Templates on page 16 for instructions and illustrations.) To use a template, you place it atop the wrong side (the back) of the fabric and use a fabric marker to trace around it. That transfers the shape onto the fabric, making the shape easy to cut out and use. (You'll have a chance to practice this when you make Lyle the Horned Alien, following the instructions and illustrations on pages 16-20.) Make your tracings close together and as close to the edges of the fabric as possible, keeping in mind that you'll usually need to cut out more pieces later. (You don't want to run out of fabric.)

Always use a fabric pen or a pencil to trace your templates onto your fabric. (Pencils work best on light-colored or thin fabrics where you really don't want any ink to show.) Don't use any ink that bleeds. The moment your monster gets wet, the ink creates stains.

Sewing Techniques & Terms

Right Sides Together

You'll see this term often in the instructions. As you arrange your pieces of fabric to sew seams, you'll always place them with their "**right sides together.**" This means you lay them with the prettiest or fuzziest sides facing each other. That's because you want to sew on the "wrong" sides so

that your seams will be hidden when the fabric is turned right side out again.

Felt has no "wrong" side, but other fabrics have a different texture or pattern on each side. The right side of faux fur has a pile, which just means the direction the fur likes to "grow." In general, you will want your fur to "grow" down, but it may be fun to sew it so that it "grows" up, too.

Pinning

You'll use the pins to **pin** the fabric wherever corners meet and wherever you intend to sew a seam. This holds everything in place until you are ready to sew. To pin, match the edges of your fabric that you intend to stitch. Working perpendicular to the fabric's edges, send the pin's sharp tip through both layers of fabric about ¼ inch (6 mm) from the edges. Push the pin's tip back up through both layers of fabric, exiting around 1/16 inch (2 mm) from your original entry point. Use one pin every two or three inches (5-7.6 mm).

Pinning

Correct   Incorrect

Here's the most important instruction about pinning: after sewing, remove the pins! You'll sew over the pins, or remove them as you get to them while stitching. But you must pull out the pins before you hug, use, or give away a plush monster.

Seam Allowance

Seam allowance is the distance between the seam you will sew and the edge of your fabric. A seam allowance is used to ensure the edges of your creature won't **unravel**. A ¼-inch (6 mm) seam allowance is standard for most of the plush monsters in this book. Each set of instructions tells you what seam allowance to leave.

Right Sides Together

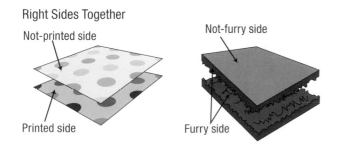

Not-printed side

Printed side

Not-furry side

Furry side

Threading a Needle

The first step to sewing is threading the needle you'll use. Grab a needle. Use the fabric scissors to cut a 20-inch (50.8 cm) length of thread. Pass one end of the thread through the needle's eye (that's the opening at the top). If the thread splits and won't go through the eye, moisten your fingers, pinch and twist the end, and try again. If that fails, snip off that end and try again with the new end. Once you get it through, pull enough of the thread to create a 4-inch (10.2 cm) tail.

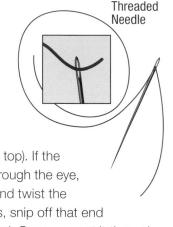

Threaded Needle

One more thing: you must make sure the thread stays in the fabric, and you can do this by **anchoring** it. Take your threaded needle and stitch up from the wrong side of the fabric, leaving an inch or two of tail on the wrong side (1). Stitch down into the right side of the fabric and pull the thread taut but not so tight that you pull the tail through (2). Stitch back up from the wrong side (3). Repeat six to eight times, until the tail does not budge when you pull the thread taut. Your thread is securely anchored.

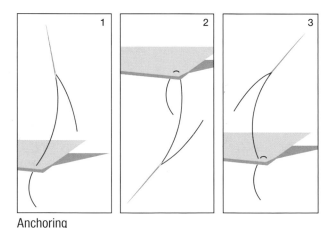

Anchoring

Assembly

Assembly is when you put together the pieces of your monster. Often you'll sew pieces together, and then sew them to more pieces. Completed arms, legs, horns, and ears are generally sewn into the seams of the body when the right sides of the body are together. Warning: your creature looks its freakiest at this stage. Its appendages are positioned so that they are facing inward, **sandwiched** between the two facing right sides of the fabric. In fact, this technique of layering pieces is called sandwiching, and you'll see that term often. Later, the whole monster is turned right side out. Reaching this step means you are close to finishing. Don't be surprised if your monster begins drooling with anticipation.

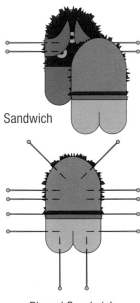

Sandwich

Pinned Sandwich

Backstitch

The **backstitch** is a hand-sewing method for creating a seam. It's a good stitch, so most of the creatures shown in this book were sewn with backstitches. Anytime you're not sure what kind of stitch to use, go ahead and use a backstitch.

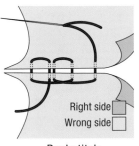

Right side
Wrong side

Backstitch

To backstitch, grab a threaded needle and two layers of fabric you want to join. Push in the needle from behind/ underneath the fabric so the knot is on the wrong side. (Be sure to leave the proper seam allowance.)

Push the needle all the way through and pull until the knot touches the fabric. Then send your needle back through both layers, about ⅛ inch (3 mm) in front of where the needle came through. Push the needle into the other side again so that it comes up through the middle of your original stitch. Pull the thread taut, and make another stitch the same length as the first one, reentering the fabric at a point beyond the end of your original stitch. Your stitches on the underside will be twice as long as those on the upper side. Repeat this process until you have completed your seam.

Straight Stitch

This stitch is as basic as it sounds. A **straight stitch** draws a single thread in a straight line through the front side of the fabric and then back down through. This hand-sewing technique is suggested for making a few of the plush creatures in this book.

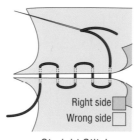

Right side
Wrong side

Straight Stitch

Do You Have a Sewing Machine?

Lucky you! Though the project instructions explain how to make these friendly beasts as if you are sewing by hand, you can use a sewing machine instead. Just follow the manufacturer's directions for setting up and using the machine.

Unless you want to get fancy, set the machine to use a straight stitch (at zero-stitch width) for all sewing unless the directions specify using a **zigzag stitch**. (Read more about zigzag stitches and see one on page 15.) For a zigzag stitch, select a medium-to-wide stitch width.

A few of the projects recommend using a sewing machine because you'll be sewing through many layers. A machine makes the work easier, so do yourself a favor and team up with a friend who owns and knows how to use a sewing machine to create those critters.

Whipstitch

The **whipstitch** is a hand-sewing technique used to bind edges to prevent unraveling. It's recommended for closing up your creature when you are finished stuffing it. It's easy. Just stab your needle through your fabric, roughly ⅛ to 1/16 inch (3 to 1.5 mm) from the edge, and pull

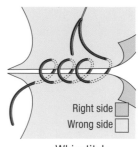

Right side
Wrong side

Whipstitch

it out the other side. Loop the thread over the fabric's edge and reenter on the same side of the fabric you entered before, as close as you can (1/16 inch [1.5 mm] or closer). Send the needle all the way through, and then repeat the process.

Appliqué

Appliqué means to apply one layer of fabric over another to create a design or pattern. The fabric pieces sewn on top are called appliqués, and they don't require seam allowances. (To see an example, look at The Juju Triplets on page 22. They have appliquéd faces.) To appliqué, lay your appliqué piece right side up on top of the right side of the background fabric. Straight stitch around the edges of the appliqué to attach it, unless the instructions recommend another stitch.

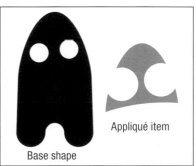

Base shape

Appliqué item

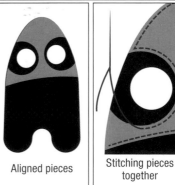

Aligned pieces

Stitching pieces together

Appliqué

Tying Off a Stitch

You need to secure the thread in place every time you finish sewing a seam or appliquéing. Do this by **tying off** your last stitch. Here's how: when you've made your last stitch (1), take the needle through the fabric again right on top of that stitch (2)—but this time, when you pull the thread back through, pull it through the loop of thread you just created (3). That makes a knot. Repeat this two to three times, making knots on top of knots (4). Pull them tight, and then snip off the thread near the knots (5). (If using a sewing machine, use a back-tacking technique to achieve the same effect. Refer to your sewing machine's user manual to answer any questions you have about using it.)

After you've tied off the stitch, you can remove the pins that held the fabrics in place.

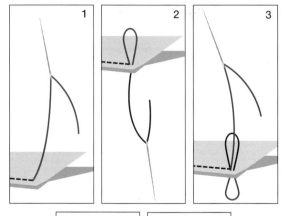

Tying Off

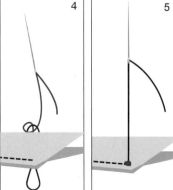

Notching

You'll sew some curves, such as a seam that goes up one leg, around, and down the other. But when you turn your monster-in-the-making right side out again, you'll notice the seam looks bunched up. Yikes! You can prevent this. Just notch the fabric of the seam allowance at the curve BEFORE you turn your plushie right side out.

Here's how: cut little ⅛-inch (3 mm) V-shapes or slits in the seam allowance along the curve, cutting from the edge of the fabric nearest the seam. Be careful not to cut the seam itself. (See figure 6C on page 18.) This relieves the pull on the fabric that can cause bunching.

Sewing on Button Eyes

You can attach a button eye before or after your monster is stuffed. The sewing technique is the same. Thread a needle with upholstery thread. Poke the needle into the fabric in the spot where you want the eye. Pull the needle through the material and back out. Loop the end of the thread several times and tie it in a knot (1). Then poke the needle up into a buttonhole and slide the button down toward the fabric (2). Stitch down through

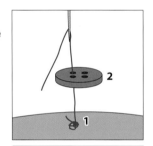

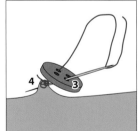

Sewing on a Button

another buttonhole and into the fabric, beginning to pull the button against the material (3). Repeat, moving the needle up through each buttonhole and down through the fabric (4) several more times. When the button feels very secure, tie off the stitch.

Zigzag Stitch

The zigzag stitch is typically a sewing machine stitch. It's a good technique for attaching facial features. It's also useful if you have a raw edge that you want to bind to prevent it from unraveling. A few of the monsters in this book were made using this stitch on some

Zigzag Stitch

parts. If you don't have a sewing machine, you can make the same stitch by hand. Making small corners with acute angles makes the zigzag pattern, so the thread forms a pattern like a series of Ms or Ws.

All About Turning Out & Stuffing

What It Means to Turn Out a Plushie

You aren't abandoning your creature! You're just turning the fabric from wrong side to right side—so you can see the outside of it. Always turn the fabric gently and use a capped pen with a round point to make sure all the edges turn. This is generally the second-to-last step in monster making.

If your critter has appendages that are sandwiched between right sides during an assembly step, however, the instructions will tell you to turn out each appendage before stuffing it separately and then sewing it to the body. That's because you are finished with the construction of that arm, leg, wing, or whatever it is. The final step in monster making is stuffing.

Here's How to Stuff

Stuffing is fun. You see your creation expanding with every bit of polyester you feed it! Stuffing is also a skill. You don't want a lumpy plush creature, right? So use small pieces of stuffing at a time. Push it in gently. Never cram. For stuffing narrow places that you can't reach with your fingers, use the eraser end of an unsharpened pencil. Stuff the beastie only as firmly as needed to maintain its shape. If the seams bulge even a little bit, unstuff!

Practice the Skills— Make a Monster

Lyle the Horned Alien Lands in Your Neighborhood

You Will Need

- Patterns (page 16)
- Basic Beastie Kit (page 8)
- Red faux fur, 8 x 5 inches (20.3 x 12.7 cm)
- Orange fleece, 10 x 7 inches (25.4 x 17.8 cm)
- 3 child-safe cat eyes

Use the fabrics and colors noted on the patterns and the supplies list, or use whatever fabrics you like.

Making Templates

1 Photocopy the patterns onto the paper. The dashed lines remind you to leave a seam allowance when you sew, and show the actual dimensions of the finished project. Don't transfer the dashed lines to your fabric when tracing your patterns.

2 Use the craft scissors to cut the copied pattern shapes from the paper. (See figure 1A.) Tape the pieces to the card stock. (See figure 1B.)

3 Cut the shapes from the card stock. (See figure 1C.) You've just made your templates. (See figure 1D.)

PATTERNS

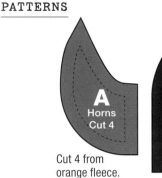

Lyle
enlarge 200%

Cut 4 from orange fleece.

Cut 2 from red faux fur.

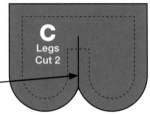

This line is for reference only. Do not cut this line into your pattern.

Cut 2 from orange fleece.

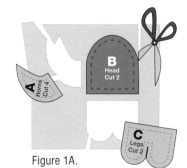

Figure 1A.

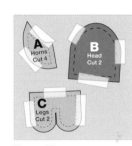

Figure 1B.

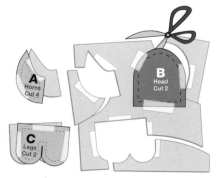

Figure 1C.

Figure 1D.

Using a Template to Cut out the Heads

① Lay the head template (the pattern shape labeled **B**) atop the wrong side of the fur. See the "cut 2 from red faux fur" note on the pattern? That means you'll be tracing and cutting out two head shapes from this fabric. Lay out this first head on the fabric so there's room for a second one. Use the fabric pen to trace the shape onto the fabric.

② Repeat step 1 to trace the second head piece. **(See figure 2A.)**

③ Use the fabric scissors to cut both pieces from the fabric. **(See figure 2B.)** These pieces will become the front and the back of the alien's head.

Figure 2A.

Figure 2B.

Using a Template to Cut out the Legs

① Lay the legs template (the pattern shape labeled **C**) atop the wrong side of the fleece. (Most fleece has no right or wrong side, but instead has two sides with slightly different textures. The side you like less can be the "wrong" side.) Notice the "cut 2 from orange fleece" note on the pattern. That means you'll be tracing and cutting out two shapes from this fabric. Lay out this first legs shape on the fabric so

there's room for a second one. Use the fabric pen to trace the shape onto the fabric.

② Repeat step 1 to trace the legs (C) template a second time. **(See figure 3A.)**

③ Use the fabric scissors to cut both pieces from the fabric. **(See figure 3B.)** Now's the time to cut between the legs, using the reference line you see in the pattern. These pieces will become the front and the back of Lyle's legs.

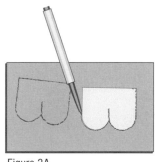

Figure 3A.

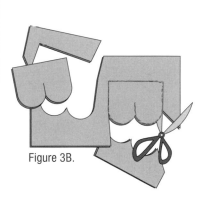

Figure 3B.

Attaching the Child-Safe Eyes

① Grab one of the head pieces. This will be the front of the head. Turn it wrong side up. Use the fabric pen to make three marks where you want the eyes to go. Just don't place the eyes too close to the edges or it will be hard to sew the pieces together. Be careful also not to mark the eyeholes too close together or the eyes might crowd each other. **(See figure 4A.)**

Figure 4A.

2 On each mark, use the fabric scissors to snip a small hole no wider than the shaft of the eye you'll insert there. It's easiest to cut from the wrong side of the fabric.

3 Insert an eye into an eyehole so that the shaft pokes through to the wrong side of the fabric. Secure the washer on the shaft by sliding it all the way to the base, snugly against the fabric. **(See figure 4B.)** Some eye shafts have ridges that snap. Others are smooth. Make sure the washer is tightly clamped as far down the shaft as possible. Repeat this step to attach the other eyes.

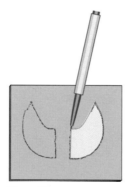

Figure 4B.

Using a Template to Cut out the Horns

1 Lay the horn template (the pattern shape labeled **A**) atop the wrong side of the orange fleece. Use the fabric pen to trace the shape onto the fabric. Flip the template and trace it onto the fabric again. You should have two mirror-image horn shapes. These shapes are the parts you'll need for one horn.

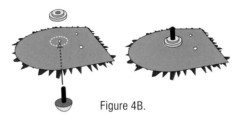

Figure 5A.

2 Repeat these steps to trace the parts for the second horn. **(See figure 5A.)** Remember, you don't have to make a flipped-backward template. Just flip the template you have.

3 Use the fabric scissors to cut out all four horn pieces.

Now Make the Horns

1 Align each pair of horn pieces, right sides together. **(See figure 6A.)** Pin the horns together.

2 Leaving a ⅜-inch (9.5 mm) seam allowance, use the needle and thread to backstitch along the two curved edges, leaving the straight edge open. **(See figure 6B.)** If sewing by hand, secure your thread with knots at the beginning and the end of your seam. (See the Anchoring illustration on page 12.) If you're using a sewing machine, secure your seam at the beginning and the end by sewing back and forth about two stitch lengths a few times.

3 Use the fabric scissors to notch any curves and to trim the corners. This keeps the fabric from bunching up when the horn is turned right side out. **(See figure 6C.)**

4 Gently turn the horns right side out. Use the end of a capped pen with a rounded point to get the horns turned out completely.

5 Stuff the horns very lightly. **(See figure 6D.)** Leave the straight edges open—don't sew them yet. Set the horns aside.

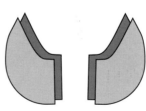

Figure 6A.

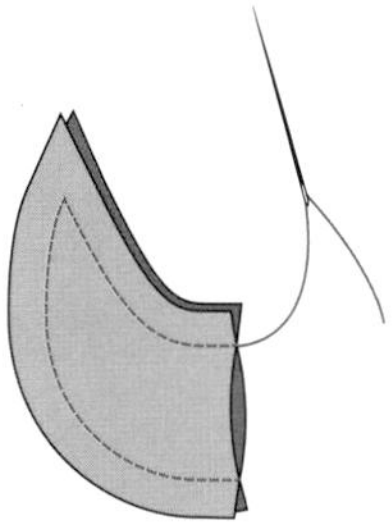

Figure 6B.

Figure 6C.

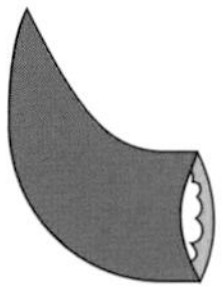

Figure 6D.

Assembling Lyle's Body

(1) Take a head piece and lay it wrong side down with its neck edge (the straight edge) at the top and the curved side at the bottom. **(See figure 7A.)**

(2) Take a legs piece and lay it right side down atop the head piece with its straight edge aligned to the straight edge of the head piece. Use straight pins to secure the two layers at the corners. Insert the pins perpendicular to the aligned edges. **(See figure 7B.)**

(3) Leaving a ¼-inch (6 mm) seam allowance, backstitch the pieces together. **(See figure 7C.)**

(4) Repeat these steps with the other head piece and the other legs piece. You've just assembled the front and back of the alien's body.

Figure 7A.

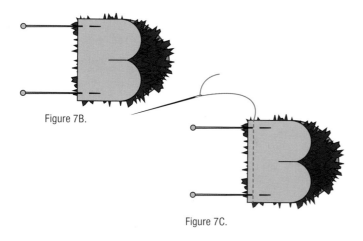

Figure 7B.

Figure 7C.

Sandwiching Lyle

(1) We're going to make a sandwich now. Start by laying the assembled front of the alien (with the eyes) right side up with the head at the top. **(See figure 8A.)**

(2) Grab the stuffed horns. Decide where on the head you think the horns ought to go. Then align the open edges of the horns with the side edges of the alien's head. You'll need to lay each horn over Lyle's face as if he's playing peek-a-boo with you. Then pin in place. **(See figure 8B.)**

(3) Lay the assembled back of the alien, right side down, atop the alien's front and horns, sandwiching the horns between the two layers of the alien. **(See figure 8C.)** Secure the layers with pins. Make sure you also pin the layers together at their neck/waist seams. **(See figure 8D.)**

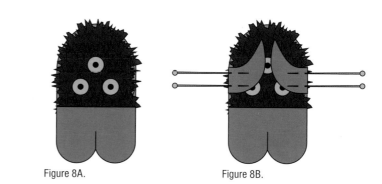

Figure 8A.

Figure 8B.

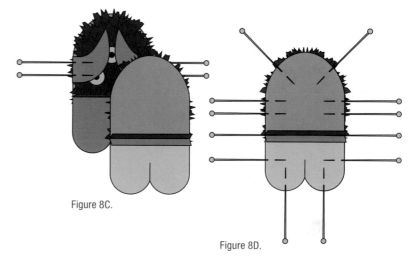

Figure 8C.

Figure 8D.

4 Use your needle and thread to backstitch all the way around the perimeter of the alien, securing the horns into place as you stitch. Leave a ¼-inch (6 mm) seam allowance. Leave a 2-inch (5 cm) opening at the top of the alien's head, or anywhere on the head that you like. Notch the seam allowance between the legs. **(See figure 8E.)**

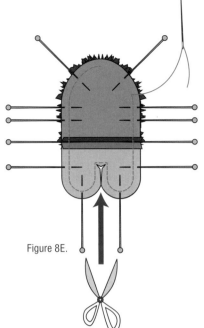

Figure 8E.

5 Remove the pins. Carefully turn the monster right side out. Use the end of a capped pen with a rounded point or a turning tool to get the head and legs turned out completely. Stuff the alien as firmly as you want. **(See figure 8F.)**

Figure 8F.

6 Time to close up the stuffing hole. Sew by hand using a whipstitch. Place the stitches very close together so you get a nice, tight seam.

Congratulations. You've made your first plush monster! Be polite: introduce Lyle to your neighbors.

Now Try This

Handy Hang Tab Instructions for Any Plush Critter

Giving your plush critter a hang tab is even better than giving it legs or wings. You can just snap your new friend on a carabineer and take it with you wherever you go. Then it'll never have trouble keeping up with you (or dodging traffic).

You Will Need

- Printed cotton fabric, 3 x 5 inches (7.6 x 12.7 cm)
- Needle and thread, or a sewing machine with universal needle and thread
- Fabric scissors
- Iron and ironing board

1 Lay your swatch right side up. Fold it long edge to long edge, right sides together. (**See figure 1.**)

Right side

Wrong side

Figure 1.

2 Leaving ¼ inch (6 mm) of seam allowance, backstitch the outside edges together. You've just made a tube. (**See figure 2.**)

3 Turn your tube right side out. Arrange the seam so that it's in the middle. (**See figure 3.**)

4 Set the iron to the cotton setting. When the iron has heated, press the tube flat with the iron. Run the iron over the tube a few times until the tube has crisp edges. (**See figure 4.**) Set the iron aside. (Leave it on to use in step 6.)

5 This hang tab needs reinforcing. So backstitch a seam about ⅛ to 3/16 inch (3 mm to 5 mm) from each long edge. This means you'll create one seam on each side of the original seam you sewed in step 2. (**See figure 5.**)

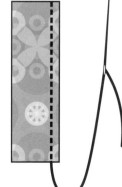
Figure 2.

Figure 3.

Figure 4.

6 Fold the tab short edge to short edge, concealing the original seam. Use the iron to press the fold down. You want to create a crisp fold. (**See figure 6.**)

7 When you're ready to attach this hang tab to a plush creature, align the loose edges (opposite the fold) with the opening you left in the creature's head. Whipstitch the hole closed and the tab in place.

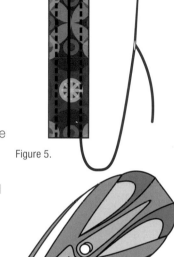
Figure 5.

Figure 6.

You've made your first hang tab (and maybe even attached it to a monster friend already). If you want or need a longer or thicker hang tab, just start with a larger swatch of fabric and use this same technique.

Do you hear those sirens? Your neighbors are boarding up windows and the streets are empty. The plush monsters have arrived...

Juju Triplets Erupt from Mt. Vesuvius

Juju Triplets' Instructions

You Will Need

- Patterns (page 25)
- Basic Beastie Kit (page 8)
- Two styles or colors of printed cotton, 8 x 8 inches (20.3 x 20.3 cm) of each fabric for each creature
- Fleece or felt in two colors, 8 x 8 inches (20.3 x 20.3 cm) of each color for each creature
- Thin cotton or polyester fabric, at least 2 ⅛ x 2 ¾ inches (5.3 x 6.9 cm) for each set of appendages (ears, horns, wings)
- 2 pairs of buttons or 1 pair of child-safe doll eyes for each creature

Use the fabrics and colors noted on the patterns and the supplies list, or use whatever fabrics you like. The triplets you see all use cotton or polyester for front pieces and hang tabs and fleece or felt for back pieces. The symbols are felt.

Making and Using Templates

1. The hardest step is deciding which triplet you'll make first. Use the patterns to create templates for that critter. Trace and cut the pieces from the wrong side of the fabrics. For the appendages (B, C, or D), remember to cut two pieces and then flip the template before cutting the final two pieces. Set all the pieces aside.

2. Draw a symbol no larger than 1 ½ x 1 ½ inches (3.8 x 3.8 cm). This is for your creature's chest. (Copy one of the symbols you see in the photo of the triplets, or create an original design.) Create a template. Trace and cut the shape from the wrong side of the fabric. Set it aside.

This monster wants to watch you work. The least you can do is go ahead and give it a face and eyes.

Appliquéing the Face and Body

1. Attach the face (F, G, or H) to the front of the head (E) using the appliqué technique (page 13).

2. Sew the eyes on the front of the head. If you are using buttons, put the larger ones underneath the smaller ones before you sew them on.

3. Appliqué the symbol to the front of the body.

4. If you started with Stinkish, you'll see that it has teeth and a tongue made from fleece. To create the teeth, cut two small, lopsided triangles out of fabric. To make a tongue, cut out a small U-shape from fabric. Sandwich the teeth and tongue between Stinkish's face and head. Appliqué it all together.

Finko

5 If you like, use a straight stitch to create a pattern on each face.

Attaching the Head to the Body

1 Grab the front head (the **E** piece with the face attached) and the front body (the **A** piece with the symbol attached). Working with the wrong sides face up, align the lower edge of the head to the neck of the body. Pin in place.

2 Backstitch the bottom edge of the head to the top edge of the body. Leave a ³⁄₁₆- to ¼-inch (5 to 6 mm) seam allowance at this attachment. Set the sewn piece aside.

3 Repeat steps 1 and 2 to join the back of the head (the other **E** piece) and the back of the body (the other **A** piece). Set the sewn piece aside.

Your creature is beginning to look like…a creature.

Making Ears, Horns, and Wings

1 Match the appendages, rights sides together, to create a pair of ears, horns, or wings (**B**, **C**, or **D**). Leaving a ¼-inch (6 mm) seam allowance, backstitch one appendage together, leaving the straight edge open. (The straight edge is where the appendage will attach to the head.) Repeat for the second appendage.

2 Notch any curves or corners. Flip the appendage right side out, and lightly stuff it. Or don't stuff it. It's up to you. Repeat for the other ear, horn, or wing you've sewn.

3 You can use a straight stitch to create a pattern on each appendage, if you like.

Your triplet is minutes away from completion. Are you ready to finish it?

Sewing Up Your Creature

1 Sandwich the appendages between the front and back of the head. The body will be wrong side out and the appendages will be right side out inside the head. (See diagram.)

2 Pin all the edges.

3 Leaving a ¼-inch (6 mm) seam allowance, backstitch from the top of the head down one side of the body and back around to the other side, back up to the top of the head. (See the stitching lines on the diagram.) Leave an opening in the middle of the top of the head so you can stuff your creature.

4 If you haven't already, go ahead and remove all the pins. Carefully turn your triplet right side out. Stuff it as firmly as you want.

5 Make and attach the hang tab and sew up the opening. (See Handy Hang Tab Instructions on pages 20-21.)

Now, make the other triplets. Hang them from your keychain, carabineer, or Christmas tree.
Beware of bursts of lava.

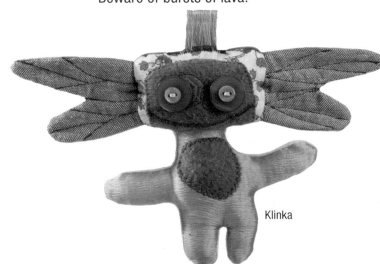

Klinka

PATTERNS

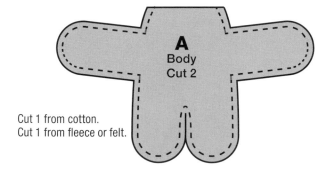

A
Body
Cut 2

Cut 1 from cotton.
Cut 1 from fleece or felt.

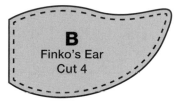

B
Finko's Ear
Cut 4

Cut 2 from thin cotton or polyester.
Cut 2 from fleece or felt.

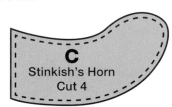

C
Stinkish's Horn
Cut 4

Cut 2 from thin cotton or polyester.
Cut 2 from fleece or felt.

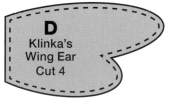

D
Klinka's
Wing Ear
Cut 4

Cut 2 from thin cotton or polyester.
Cut 2 from fleece or felt.

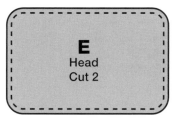

E
Head
Cut 2

Cut 1 from cotton.
Cut 1 from fleece or cotton.

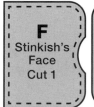

F
Stinkish's
Face
Cut 1

Cut 1 from
fleece or felt.

G
Klinka's
Face
Cut 1

Cut 1 from fleece
or felt.

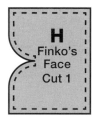

H
Finko's
Face
Cut 1

Cut 1 from fleece
or felt.

DIAGRAM

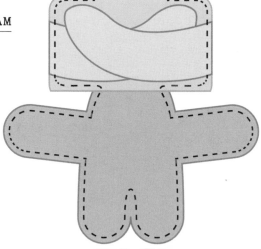

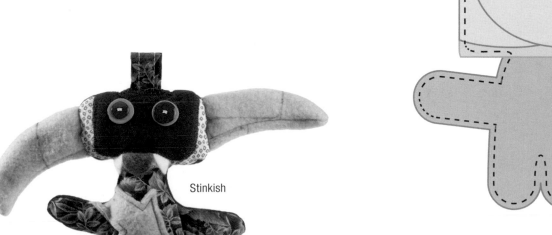

Stinkish

25

Split-Personality Beamed to Earth

Billions view its moody arrival via live broadcasts

Split-Personality's Instructions

You Will Need

- Patterns (page 29)
- Basic Beastie Kit (page 8)
- Red fleece, 7 x 7 inches (17.8 x 17.8 cm)
- Orange fleece, 7 x 7 inches (17.8 x 17.8 cm)
- Yellow fleece, 7 x 7 inches (17.8 x 17.8 cm)
- Green fleece, 7 x 7 inches (17.8 x 17.8 cm)
- Blue fleece, 7 x 7 inches (17.8 x 17.8 cm)
- Black felt, 7 x 7 inches (17.8 x 17.8 cm)
- White felt, 4 x 3 inches (10.2 x 7.6 cm)
- Polyester thread in black and white

Use the fabrics and colors noted on the patterns and the supplies list, or use whatever fabrics you like.

Making and Using Templates

1 Use the patterns to create the templates. Use the pencil to trace and cut each shape from the wrong side of the fabrics. (The Split-Personality plushie you see has felt eyes, teeth, and mouth. The rest is fleece.) Set the pieces aside.

Give this character a grin and a grimace.

Making Faces

1 Pin the eyebrows (D), large black eye (E) pieces, teeth (H), and smile (I) to the right sides of the yellow and green fabric that make up the body pieces. (See the diagrams for placement.) Don't pin the white eye pieces (F) and small black eye pieces (G) yet because you won't be able to sew what goes beneath them.

2 Use black thread for the eyebrows, large black eye pieces, and the smile. Whipstitch those facial features in place. (If using a sewing machine, use a zigzag stitch on all pieces. Or, if you like the way zigzag stitches look, zigzag stitch by hand.)

3 Center the white eye (**F**) pieces atop the large black eye (**E**) pieces and pin in place. Use white thread to whipstitch the white eye pieces and the teeth (**H**) in place, sewing all the way into the body piece. (If using a sewing machine, use a zigzag stitch.)

4 Center the small black eye pieces (**G**) atop the whites of the eyes. Use black thread to whipstitch the small black eye pieces in place, sewing all the way into the body piece. (If using a sewing machine, use a zigzag stitch.)

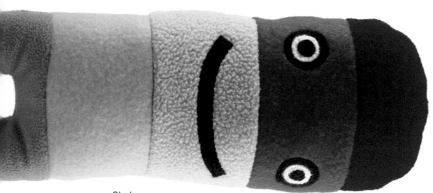
Glad

Constructing the Body

1 Line up the pieces of the front body (one set of **A**, **B**, and **C** pieces, including the glad face), laying them flat and aligning them so the long straight edges touch. Working with two pieces at a time, pin them right sides together along the edges. (So, pin red to orange, then pin orange to yellow, and so on.) Repeat this step for the back body (one set of **A**, **B**, and **C** pieces, including the mad face).

2 Backstitch the front body pieces together, leaving a ⅜-inch (9.5 mm) seam allowance. Set the front body aside. Repeat this step for the back body.

This plushie is so close to being finished you may hear a giggle—or is that a growl?

Sewing up Your Creature

1 Pin the front and back body pieces, right sides together. Make sure the color panels match up on the sides, where you'll sew the seams.

2 Leaving a ¼-inch (6 mm) seam allowance, backstitch along the edges. Leave a 2-inch (5 cm) opening in the creature's side for turning and stuffing.

3 If you haven't already, now's the time to remove all the pins. Notch the curves around the top and between the legs.

4 Carefully turn your monster right side out. Stuff it as firmly as you want. Sew the opening closed.

Sad? Turn to its glad side for a dose of contagious cheeriness. Angry? Challenge the mad side to a stare-down. See who cracks a smile first.

Mad

PATTERNS

A
Head
Cut 2

Cut 2 from red fleece.

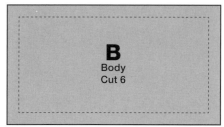

B
Body
Cut 6

Cut 2 from orange fleece.
Cut 2 from yellow fleece.
Cut 2 from green fleece.

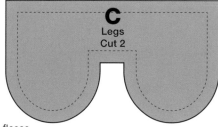

C
Legs
Cut 2

Cut 2 from blue fleece.

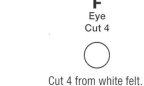

D
Eyebrow
Cut 2

Cut 2 from black felt.

F
Eye
Cut 4

Cut 4 from white felt.

E
Large Black Eye
Cut 4

Cut 4 from black felt.

G
Small Black Eye
Cut 4

Cut 4 from black felt.

H
Teeth
Cut 1

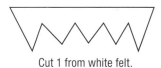

Cut 1 from white felt.

I
Smile
Cut 1

Cut 1 from black felt.

DIAGRAMS

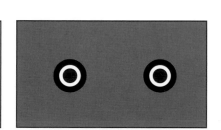

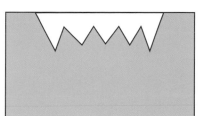

Tri-Plod's Standoff Ends Peacefully

Authorities mistake harmless sightseer for marauding menace

You Will Need

- Patterns (page 32)
- Basic Beastie Kit (page 8)
- Red felt, 1 yard (91.4 cm)
- Black faux fur, 6 x 6 inches (15.2 x 15.2 cm)
- 6 child-safe doll eyes

Use the fabrics and colors noted on the patterns and the supplies list, or use whatever fabrics you like.

Making and Using Templates

1 Use the patterns to create templates. Trace and cut your pieces from the wrong side of the fabrics. (Felt has no wrong side, but the faux fur and any other fabric you may use do.) Set the pieces aside.

Make some room to lay out the parts of this dinosaur-like beast.

Constructing the Body

1 Lay out the three body (A) pieces. Align the tops of the heads from nose to crown so the pieces are just touching edges, not overlapping. (For fabrics other than felt, right sides should be facing down.) This leaves a triangle-shaped gap between the crowns. Pin the pieces together where they touch.

2 Place the hair (B) piece fur-side down over the triangle-shaped gap, making sure its edges overlap onto each body piece. Pin along those edges.

3 Leaving a ¼-inch (6 mm) seam allowance, backstitch the pieces together where you pinned. It's easiest to get started by poking your needle through the fuzzy side of the hair piece.

4 Match the remaining edges of the body pieces. Pin the pieces where they touch.

5 Backstitch from each nose down to the leg on that side, stopping 2 inches (5 cm) from the underside where the body pieces meet. (This opening will be your turning and stuffing hole.)

6 Now's the time to remove all the pins. Notch the curves and corners.

Tri-Plod has six inquisitive, unblinking eyes. Two on each head.

Attaching the Eyes

1 Grab one of Tri-Plod's heads. Use the fabric pen to make a mark 1½ inches (3.8 cm) from the tip of the nose, equidistant from each seam. (This mark will be on the wrong side of the fabric.) Repeat on the other side of the head. Repeat this step for each remaining head.

2 On each mark, snip a small hole no wider than the shaft of the eye you'll insert there.

3 Reaching into Tri-Plod through its stuffing hole, insert an eye into an eyehole so that the shaft pokes through to the wrong side of the creature. Secure the washer on the shaft. Repeat this step for each remaining eyehole.

Finishing Tri-Plod

1 Carefully turn the beast right side out. Stuff it as firmly as you want. Sew the opening closed.

Tri-Plod is a friendly, snuggly plushie. Don't be afraid to use it as a napping pillow.

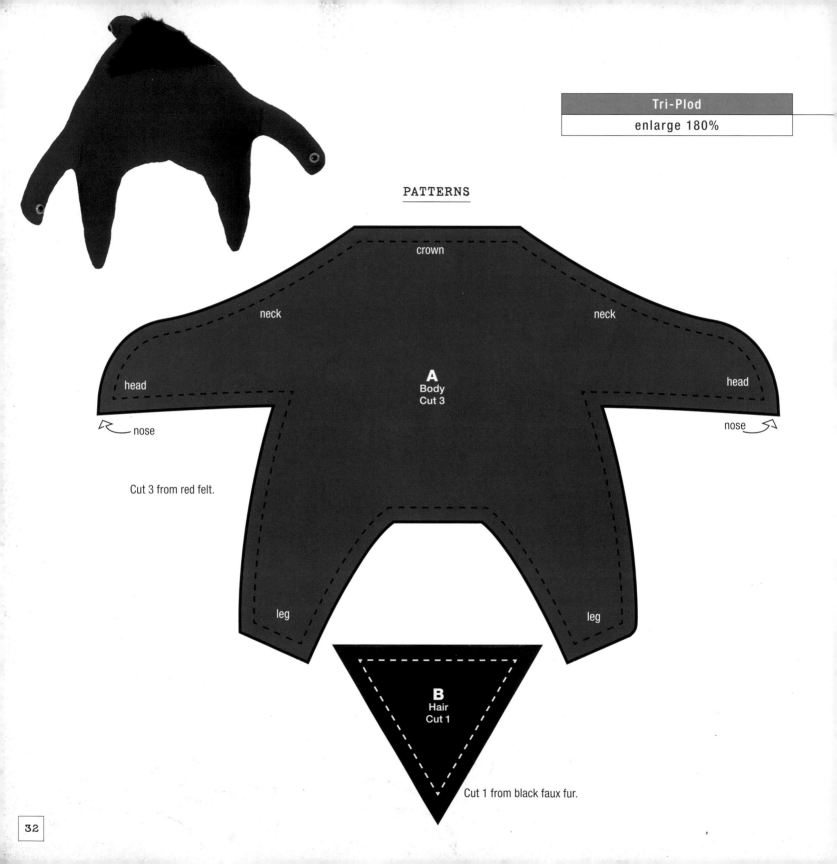

PATTERNS

crown

neck   neck

head   head

A
Body
Cut 3

nose   nose

Cut 3 from red felt.

leg   leg

B
Hair
Cut 1

Cut 1 from black faux fur.

Pocket Mouth a Power Source?

Possibilities electrify green energy advocates

You Will Need

- Patterns (page 35)
- Basics Beastie Kit (page 8)
- Green felt or fleece, 1 yard (91.4 cm)
- Red felt or fleece, 8 x 8 inches (20.3 x 20.3 cm)
- 2 triangular buttons for eyes plus 2 round black buttons, or a pair of child-safe doll eyes

Use the fabrics and colors noted on the patterns and the supplies list, or use whatever fabrics you like.

Making and Using Templates

1 Use the patterns to create templates. Trace and cut your pieces. If you use fleece, cut all pieces from the wrong side of the fabrics. Cut two of the body (A) pieces. Then flip the template and cut two more pieces. Set the pieces aside.

Put down the scissors. Pick up your pins.

Starting the Body

1 Grab two body (A) pieces to form the back body. Lay them flat and align them so the short, curved sides touch. (See diagram.) Put the right sides of that edge together. Pin the pieces where they touch. Repeat this step for the front body.

2 Backstitch the pieces together, just stitching along this one side, leaving a ¼-inch (6 mm) seam allowance. Set it aside. Repeat this step for the front body.

Pocket Mouth needs a pocket.

Making the Pocket

1 Choose any edge of the pocket (B) to be the top. Fold that edge down 1½ inch (3.8 cm). (If you're working with fleece, fold the pocket's edge against the wrong side of the fabric.) Backstitch the folded edge to the rest of the pocket, leaving a ¼-inch (6 mm) seam allowance. This creates a hem.

2 Repeat step 1 for the bottom and side edges of the pocket, but only fold the fabric down ½ inch (1.3 cm). (Look at the photo of the finished creature to see the snazzy effect of having different hem widths.) You now have a pocket that's ready to be attached.

3 Center the pocket fold-side-down on top of the front body piece. Pin in place. Leaving a ¼-inch (6 mm) seam allowance to create a nice hem, backstitch the pocket's sides and bottom to the front body.

Attaching the Eyes

1 Grab your buttons. Stack them in pairs, arranged however you'd like the eyes to look. Then sew one stacked pair of buttons just above the top right corner of the pocket (B). Sew the second stack of buttons just above the top left corner of the pocket. (See page 14 for tips on sewing on button eyes.)

Finishing the Body

1 Pin the front and back body pieces together. (Pin right sides together.)

2 Leaving a ¼-inch (6 mm) seam allowance, backstitch along the edges. Leave a 2-inch (5 cm) opening at the bottom of the creature for turning and stuffing.

3 If you haven't already, now's the time to remove all the pins. Notch any curves or corners. Carefully turn your monster right side out. Stuff it as firmly as you want. Sew the opening closed.

This beastie is ready for hugging— if you've removed the pins!

PATTERNS

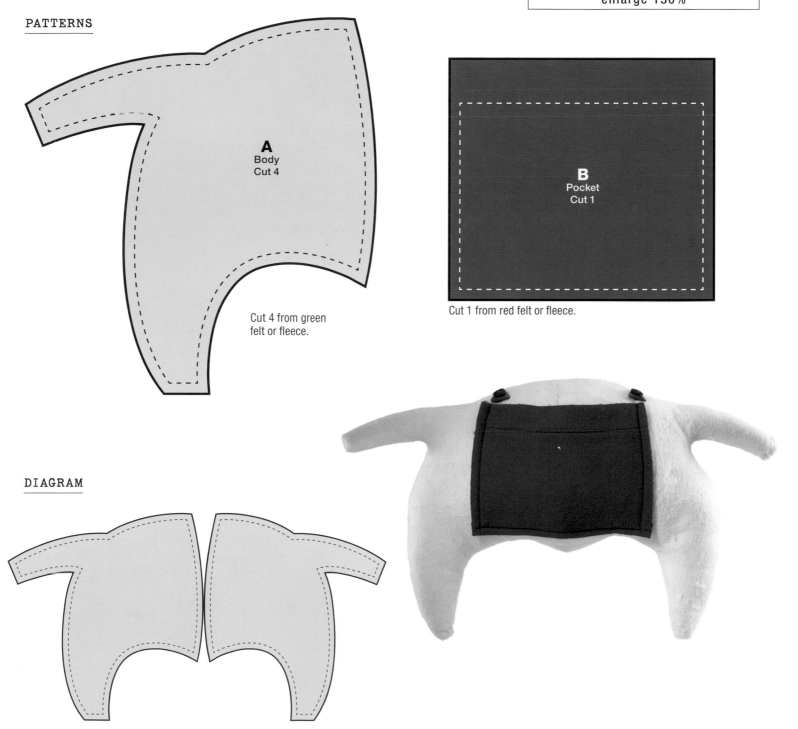

A
Body
Cut 4

Cut 4 from green
felt or fleece.

B
Pocket
Cut 1

Cut 1 from red felt or fleece.

DIAGRAM

Cosmic Three Vacation in Canyons

Cosmic Three's Instructions

You Will Need

- Patterns (page 39)
- Basic Beastie Kit (page 8)
- Two contrasting colors of fleece, 8 x 8 inches (20.3 x 20.3 cm), for each alien
- Fleece in a third color, 3 x 2 inches (7.6 x 5 cm), for each alien
- White felt, 2 x 2 inches (5 x 5 cm) (optional, for teeth)
- 2 to 3 child-safe doll eyes or cat eyes per alien

Use the fabrics and colors noted on the patterns and the supplies list, or use whatever you like.

Making and Using Templates

1. Decide which of the Cosmic Three you want to make first. Use the patterns to create templates for that alien. Trace and cut all your pieces from the wrong side of the fabrics.

Simple appliqués make each of these aliens unique. They like it that way.

Appliquéing the Face and Body

1. Making Floaty? Grab one of its body (**A**) pieces. Turn it right side up, with the rounded end at the top. Center the face (**E**) piece right side up over the top half of the body. Use the appliqué technique (page 13) to attach the face. Also stitch any design you like—such as lines—on Floaty's chest. Then skip to Attaching the Eyes.

2. Making Clicky? Grab one of its body (**B**) pieces. Turn it right side up, with the rounded end at the top. Align the eye pad (**F**) pieces right side up anywhere you like, or just like you see on the finished creature. (They are widely spaced, with one narrow edge of each eye pad aligning with the edge of the body.) Use the appliqué technique (page 13) to attach each eye pad.

3. Position Clicky's screen (**H**) piece right side up about ½ inch (1.3 cm) below its eye pads. Make sure it's turned lengthwise so it fits on the body. Appliqué the screen in place. Then stitch a graphic design on the screen like you see in the photo of Clicky. Appliqué a small rectangular nose shape between the eyes. Or not. Then skip to Attaching the Eyes.

4 Making Glurky? Grab one of its body **(C)** pieces. Turn it right side up, with the rounded end at the top. Measure down 2 inches (5 cm) from the rounded end and make a pencil mark there. Draw a horizontal line across Glurky's body on that mark. This is the line where you'll align the straight edges of the teeth **(I)**, right side up.

5 Use the appliqué technique (page 13) to attach the teeth **(I)** pieces, stitching a thick seam of thread atop the line you made. That line is his lip. (The bottoms of the teeth can be left loose, or can be appliquéd to the body.)

6 Place Glurky's symbol **(G)** right side up and slightly off-center just below its teeth. Appliqué the symbol in place.

These extraterrestrial explorers rely on all their senses—including their eyes— to observe strange life-forms like you.

Attaching the Eyes

1 On the wrong side of the fabric, make a mark where you'd like each eye. (Clicky's are centered on his eye pads. Floaty's are on the lower part of his face. Glurky's are not too far above his lip.)

2 On each mark, snip a small hole no wider than the shaft of the eye you'll insert there. It's easiest to cut from the wrong side of the fabric.

3 Working from the right side of the body, insert an eye into an eyehole so that the shaft pokes through to the wrong side. Secure the washer on the shaft. Repeat this step for each remaining eyehole.

Making the Arms

1 Match pairs of arm **(D)** pieces, rights sides together. Leaving a ¼-inch (6 mm) seam allowance, backstitch a pair of arm pieces together, leaving the straight edge open. (The straight edge is where the arm will attach to the body.) Repeat for the remaining arm pieces.

2 Notch the curved edges. Turn each arm right side out. Lightly stuff it. Or don't stuff it. You decide.

It's about that time. Sandwich time.

Sewing Up Your Creatures

1 Grab a creature's front body (with the eyes attached) and back body. Align them right sides together. Sandwich the arms between the body pieces anywhere 1½ to 2½ inches (3.8 to 6.4 cm) from the bottom edge of the body. (The body will be wrong side out and the appendages will be right side out inside the body.) Pin all the edges.

2 Leaving a ¼-inch (6 mm) seam allowance, backstitch from the top of the head down one side and around the body to the other side of the head. Leave an opening in the middle of the top of the head so you can stuff your alien.

3 If you haven't done so already, remove all the pins. Notch any curves or corners. Carefully turn your cosmic pal right side out. Stuff it as firmly as you want.

4 Make and attach the hang tab and sew up the opening. (See Handy Hang Tab Instructions on pages 20-21.) Repeat for the other two cosmic creatures.

Floaty   Clicky   Glurky

PATTERNS

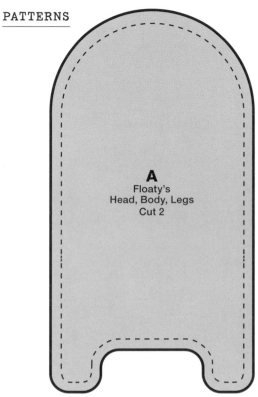

A
Floaty's
Head, Body, Legs
Cut 2

Cut 1 from fleece.
Cut 1 from fleece in a contrasting color.

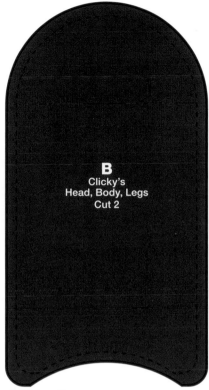

B
Clicky's
Head, Body, Legs
Cut 2

Cut 1 from fleece.
Cut 1 from fleece in a contrasting color.

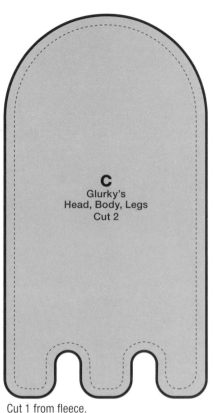

C
Glurky's
Head, Body, Legs
Cut 2

Cut 1 from fleece.
Cut 1 from fleece in a contrasting color.

E
Floaty's
Face
Cut 1

Cut 1 from the third
color of fleece.

F
Clicky's Eye
Pad
Cut 2

Cut 2 from the third
color of fleece.

I
Glurky's Teeth
Cut 3

Cut 3 from white felt.

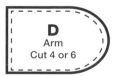

D
Arm
Cut 4 or 6

Cut 4 from any color fleece
for Floaty or Clicky.

Cut 6 from fleece for Glurky.

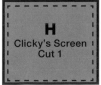

H
Clicky's Screen
Cut 1

Cut 1 from the third
color of fleece.

G
Glurky's Symbol
Cut 1

Cut 1 from the third
color of fleece.

Big Belly Inhales Everything in its Path

Officials enlist its aid as downtown fire rages

You Will Need

- Patterns (page 43)
- Basic Beastie Kit (page 8)
- White felt, 2 pieces measuring 2 x 2 inches (5 x 5 cm) each
- Green faux fur, ½ yard (45.7 cm)
- Blue fleece, ½ yard (45.7 cm)
- Black felt, 4 x 4 inches (10.2 x 10.2 cm)
- Batting, ½ yard (45.7 cm)
- Striped knit, 12 x 12 inches (30.5 x 30.5 cm)
- Polyester thread in black and white
- Two 40-mm googly eyes, or one pair of child-safe doll eyes
- Hot-glue gun and glue sticks (follow manufacturer's directions for use)

Use the fabrics and colors noted on the patterns and the supplies list, or use whatever fabrics you like.

Making and Using Templates

1 Use the patterns to create templates. For the teeth, trace the triangle (F) onto white felt three times. Leave some space between each triangle. Don't cut out these pieces yet. You'll do that later.

2 Trace and cut the other shapes from the wrong side of the fabrics. For the horns (E), cut out two pieces, and then flip the pattern to cut out another pair. Set all the pieces aside.

Time to make the face. Don't worry—Big Belly won't bite the hand that makes it.

Making the Face

1 Place the piece of white felt with the traced triangles (the teeth) atop another piece of white felt. (If using a fabric other than felt, put the pieces right sides together.) Pin the pieces together.

2 Leaving a ¼-inch seam allowance, use white thread to backstitch along two sides of the triangle for each tooth. Leave the third side open. (Back-tack if using a sewing machine.)

3 Cut out each tooth. Snip off the end of the triangle where your seam comes to a point. On the side that you did not sew, cut right on the line. Don't cut your seam end.

4 Remove the pins. Notch the corners of the teeth. Turn each tooth right side out. Set them aside.

5 Pin the eyebrows (D) to the right side of the front body piece (A). (See diagrams for placement.) Zigzag stitch the eyebrows in place using black thread. Set the piece aside.

Big Belly isn't just thick when it's full of whatever it catches in its mouth. This monster is made of layers.

Constructing the Body

1 Align the batting piece with a mouth hole (B) with the wrong side of the monster's front body (A). Make sure the batting is in the center of the front body. Use the mouth as a guide (since the batting is smaller). Pin these together.

2 Leaving a ⅜-inch (9.5 mm) seam allowance, backstitch the pieces together around the mouth opening. Leave the edges open for now.

3 Grab the blue fleece lining piece with a mouth opening (A). Align its wrong side with the batting layer and the front body. Sew following the instructions in step 2. (Don't worry, the batting won't show so long as the edges of the lining and the front body are aligned.) Set the monster's front aside.

4 Align the batting piece without an opening (B) with the wrong side of the monster's back body (A). Pin these together.

5 Leaving a ⅜-inch (9.5 mm) seam allowance, backstitch the pieces together around the edges.

6 Locate the lining piece without a mouth opening (B). Align its wrong side with the stuffing layer you just sewed to the back body. Sew following the instructions in step 5. Set the back body aside.

Making Arms, Legs, and Horns

1 For each arm/leg (C), match up a front to a back piece with right sides touching.

2 Leaving a ⅜-inch (9.5 mm) of seam allowance, backstitch the pieces together, leaving the straight edges open.

3 Notch the curves of the arms/legs. Turn them right side out. Stuff them lightly. Set the pair of arms and pair of legs aside.

4 For each horn (E), match up a front to a back piece with right sides touching.

5 Leaving a ⅜-inch (9.5 mm) of seam allowance, backstitch the pieces together, leaving the straight edges open. Set the pair of horns aside.

Now you have legs, arms, horns, and teeth lying around. Time to attach them to your creature.

Sewing up Your Creature

1 Sandwich the back body, arms/legs, horns, teeth, and front body. The body pieces should be wrong side out. The arms/legs, horns, and teeth should be right side out and touching the right sides of body pieces. (See diagrams for teeth placement.) Pin all the edges.

2 Leaving a ⅜-inch (9.5 mm) seam allowance, backstitch from the top of the head all the way around the edge of the entire creature.

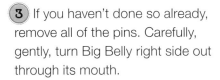

3 If you haven't done so already, remove all of the pins. Carefully, gently, turn Big Belly right side out through its mouth.

4 Now attach the eyes using a hot-glue gun.

Big Belly likes to snack on house keys and cell phones. Warn your friends. Suggest they placate this beastie by feeding it cash.

PATTERNS

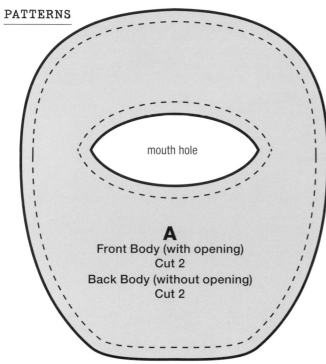

mouth hole

A
Front Body (with opening)
Cut 2
Back Body (without opening)
Cut 2

Cut 2 (1 front and 1 back) from green faux fur.
Cut 2 (1 front and 1 back) from blue fleece.

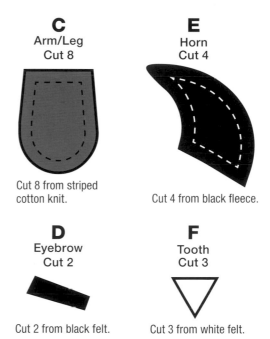

C
Arm/Leg
Cut 8

Cut 8 from striped cotton knit.

E
Horn
Cut 4

Cut 4 from black fleece.

D
Eyebrow
Cut 2

Cut 2 from black felt.

F
Tooth
Cut 3

Cut 3 from white felt.

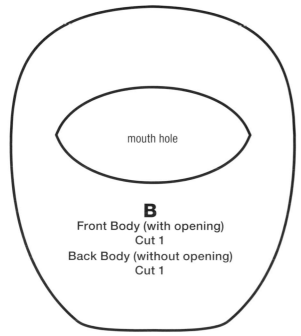

mouth hole

B
Front Body (with opening)
Cut 1
Back Body (without opening)
Cut 1

Cut 2 (1 front and 1 back) from batting.

DIAGRAMS

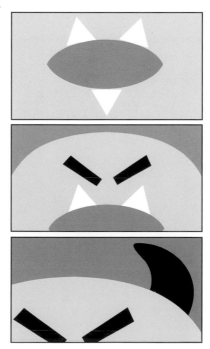

NASA Detects Alien Spaceship and Crew Orbiting Earth

See first-ever photos of Natascha, Pinko, Duopony, and Lyle

Aliens and Spaceship Instructions

You Will Need

- Patterns (pages 48-49)
- Basic Beastie Kit (page 8)
- Fuchsia fleece, 12 x 10 inches (30.5 x 25.4 cm), for Natascha
- Green faux fur, 7 x 9 inches (17.8 x 22.9 cm), for Natascha
- Hot pink faux fur, 6 x 8 inches (15.2 x 20.3 cm), for Pinko
- Turquoise fleece, 8 x 4 inches (20.3 x 10.2 cm), for Pinko
- Green fleece, 7 x 9 inches (17.8 x 22.9 cm), for Duopony
- Yellow faux fur, 13 x 6 inches (33 x 15.2 cm), for Duopony
- Gray fleece, 24 x 24 inches (61 x 61 cm)
- Light blue fleece, 15 x 11 inches (38.1 x 27.9 cm)
- Dark blue fleece, 15 x 11 inches (38.1 x 27.9 cm)
- Striped cotton knit, 15 x 11 inches (38.1 x 27.9 cm)
- Silver trim, ½ inch x 1 yard (1.3 x 91.4 cm) cut into eight 3½-inch-long (8.9 cm) pieces
- Polyester thread in light blue and black
- 12 silver buttons
- 2 to 3 child-safe cat eyes per alien

To make Lyle (the red and orange alien with horns pictured on pages 44 and 47), see instructions on pages 16-20.

Use the fabrics and colors noted on the patterns and the supplies list, or use whatever fabrics you like.

Making and Using Templates

(1) Use the patterns to create templates. Trace and cut your pieces from the wrong side of the fabrics. For Natascha's antenna (G), cut two pieces, then flip the template and cut the two remaining pieces. Set all the pieces aside.

These may be the fuzziest, cutest
aliens you've ever seen.

Making the Alien Bodies

(1) Grab all the pieces for one of the aliens. Align the head or heads (B, C, or E) to its matching legs (A, D, or F), so you have a front body and a back body. (See the layout of the patterns on page 48 for guidance.) Pin right sides together.

(2) Leaving a ⅜-inch (9.5 mm) seam allowance, backstitch the front body pieces together. Repeat, backstitching the back body pieces together. Set these pieces aside.

Making more than one alien at a time? Go ahead and repeat the last two steps for the other creatures now.

Making the Antenna

(1) Are you making Natascha? Align the right sides of Natascha's two pairs of antenna (G) pieces. Pin each pair together.

(2) Leaving a ⅜-inch (9.5 mm) seam allowance, backstitch each antenna's pieces together, leaving the straight ends open.

(3) Notch the curves around the tops. Then gently turn each antenna inside out. Stuff it lightly.

Attaching the Eyes

(1) Use the fabric pen mark on the wrong side of the alien's head (either side of its B, C, or E piece), wherever you want an eye. Mark each eye you intend to attach. (Don't place the eyes too close together, or they won't fit. Also avoid getting too close to the fabric's edge—that makes it difficult to sew the seams.)

(2) On each mark, snip a small hole no wider than the shaft of the eye.

(3) Insert an eye into the hole so that the shaft pokes through to the wrong side of the creature. Secure the washer on the shaft. Repeat to attach all the eyes.

**Front body ready? Check.
Back body ready? Check. Eyes in? Check.
All systems are go for assembling your aliens.**

Sewing up Your Creatures

(1) If you're making Natascha, sandwich the body and antennae. (Duopony and Pinko have no appendages, so you can skip this step for them. Go to step 2.) The body will be wrong side out and the appendages will be right side out inside the body. Pin all the edges.

(2) Leaving a ⅜-inch (9.5 mm) seam allowance, backstitch all the way around the edge of the creature, leaving a 2-inch (5 cm) opening for turning out and stuffing.

(3) If you haven't already, remove all the pins now. Notch any curves or corners. Turn the creature right side out. Stuff it as firmly as you want. Sew the hole closed.

You've created the crew! Congratulations. Will you start planning their Earth-bound adventures, or go ahead and make their spaceship?

Starting the Spaceship

(1) Begin with the base (J) pieces. Lay them down right side up. Center one decoration (M) piece, right side up, on top of each base piece. Pin the pieces together. Use the light blue thread to backstitch along the edges of the decoration pieces. Leave no seam allowance.

(2) Grab the silver trim. Center a piece of trim over the seam you just sewed. Pin the trim in place. Use the light blue thread to straight stitch the trim to the bases, overlapping the edges of the decoration pieces. Leave no

seam allowance. Repeat with the other base pieces. Set these pieces aside.

③ Grab all of the pocket (L) pieces. Lay them right side down. Fold down the top of each pocket about ½ inch (1.3 cm) and pin in place. Use the black thread and a zigzag stitch to sew the folded edge down, leaving a ⅜-inch (9.5 mm) seam allowance. Set these pieces aside.

④ Lay the body panel (H) pieces right side up. Align a right-side-up pocket atop each body panel so the bottom edge of the pocket aligns with the bottom edge of the body panel. Pin the pockets and bases together.

⑤ Align the top of a finished base piece with the bottom of the body panel. Pin right sides together. Leaving a ⅜-inch (9.5 mm) seam allowance, backstitch the body panel, pocket, and base together. Repeat for the three remaining body panels.

Who knew a spaceship had a nose?

Attaching the Nose

① Grab the ship's nose (I) pieces. Align the bottom edge of a nose to the top edge of a body panel. Unless you don't want to alternate the colors as you see in the finished spaceship, make sure the color of the nose doesn't match the color of the base attached to the panel. Pin right sides together.

② Leaving a ⅜-inch (9.5 mm) seam allowance, backstitch the pieces together. Repeat for the remaining nose pieces and body panels.

③ Sew the buttons to the right sides of the nose pieces. (See the photos of the finished

spaceship for placement.) You now have four complete side panels for your spaceship.

You can start the countdown to blastoff now.

Assembling the Panels

① Take a side panel with a dark blue nose and place it right side up. Place a side panel with a light blue nose atop it, right side down. Pin them together. Backstitch along the long left edge.

Lyle

Natascha

Pinko

Duopony

2 Repeat step 1 with the other two side panel pieces.

3 Pin the two assembled sides of the ship, right sides together. Leaving a ⅜-inch (9.5 mm) seam allowance, backstitch the sides together, starting from the bottom of one side, stitching up to the nose, and then down the other side. Leave a 2-inch (5 cm) turning-and-stuffing hole on one side. Leave the base bottoms open.

4 Grab the underside (**K**) piece. Align it right side down with the bottom edge of the ship's base, which forms a circle. Pin together.

5 Leaving a ⅜-inch (9.5 mm) seam allowance, backstitch the underside to the edge of the base.

6 Now's the time to remove all the pins. Notch all curves and corners. Then carefully turn the ship inside out. Stuff as firmly as you like. Sew the opening closed.

When they aren't coasting through galaxies, the alien crew likes to hang out of the pockets of their ship and watch nature programs on television. They find vertebrates especially interesting.

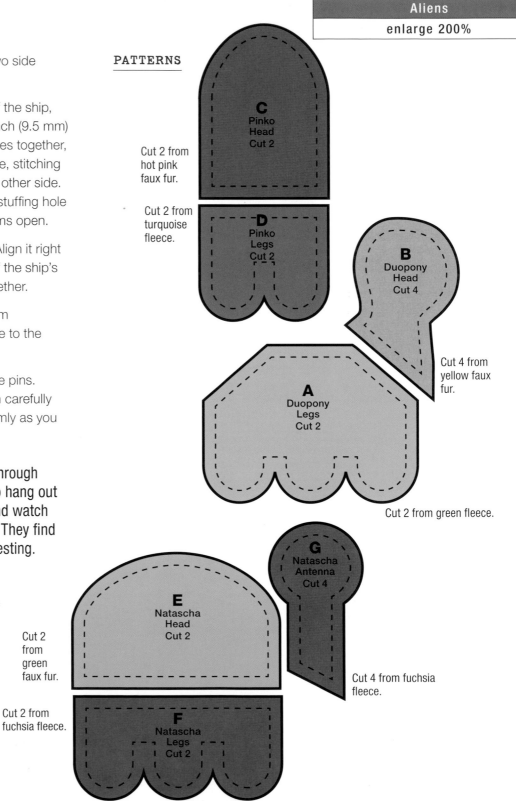

PATTERNS

C
Pinko
Head
Cut 2

Cut 2 from hot pink faux fur.

Cut 2 from turquoise fleece.

D
Pinko
Legs
Cut 2

B
Duopony
Head
Cut 4

Cut 4 from yellow faux fur.

A
Duopony
Legs
Cut 2

Cut 2 from green fleece.

G
Natascha
Antenna
Cut 4

E
Natascha
Head
Cut 2

Cut 2 from green faux fur.

Cut 2 from fuchsia fleece.

Cut 4 from fuchsia fleece.

F
Natascha
Legs
Cut 2

Aliens

enlarge 200%

Cut 2 from dark blue fleece.
Cut 2 from light blue fleece.

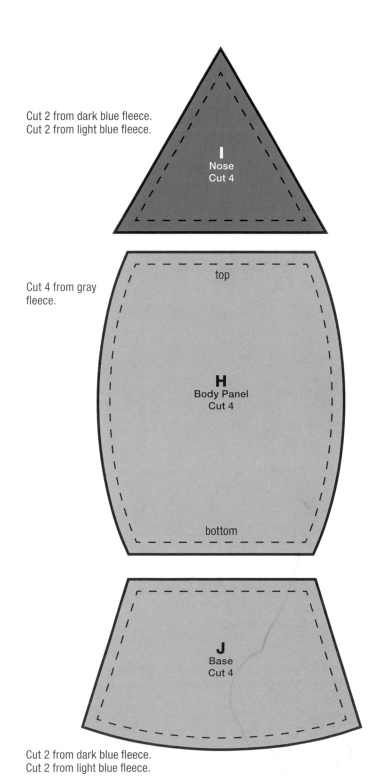

I
Nose
Cut 4

top

Cut 4 from gray fleece.

H
Body Panel
Cut 4

bottom

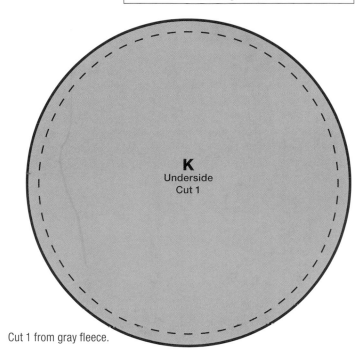

K
Underside
Cut 1

Cut 1 from gray fleece.

J
Base
Cut 4

Cut 2 from dark blue fleece.
Cut 2 from light blue fleece.

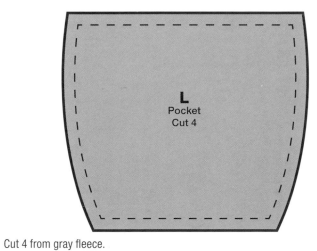

L
Pocket
Cut 4

Cut 4 from gray fleece.

M
Decoration
Cut 4

Cut 4 from striped cotton knit.

Xipp It Snacks on Freeway Overpass

Interstate closed; commuters turn to mass transit

You Will Need

- Patterns (page 53)
- Basic Beastie Kit (page 8)
- Gold felt, ½ yard (45.7 cm)
- Orange felt, 24 x 24 inches (61 x 61 cm)
- Orange zipper, 7 inches (17.8 cm) long
- 2 buttons for eyes

Use the fabrics and colors noted on the patterns and the supplies list, or use whatever fabrics you like.

Making and Using Templates

1 Use the patterns to create templates. Trace and cut your pieces. If you use a fabric other than felt, cut all pieces from the wrong side of the fabric. Also, after cutting one back body (C) and one front body (D) piece, flip each template before cutting the remaining pieces. Set all the pieces aside.

Ready to pin and sew? Xipp It is waiting on you...

Constructing the Body

1 Grab both back body (C) pieces. Align the sides labeled torso. (For fabrics other than felt, right sides should be together.) Pin the pieces along the torso.

2 Leaving a ¼-inch (6 mm) seam allowance, backstitch the pieces together to complete that side of the body.

3 Repeat steps 1 and 2 using both front body (D) pieces.

4 Align the front and back of the body along the sides labeled arm and leg. (For fabrics other than felt, right sides should be together.) Pin the pieces together.

5 Leaving a ¼-inch (6 mm) seam allowance, backstitch the front and back bodies together. Leave the bottoms of the feet open, but sew up the inside of both legs. Leave a 2-inch (5 cm) opening between the legs for turning and stuffing.

6 Notch the fabric at the curves and corners.

This monster can stand on its own. But it needs you to finish its feet "just so."

Completing the Feet

1 Pin the fabric where the bottom edges of each foot touch. Position the pins so that the feet run front to back (toe to heel).

2 Backstitch along the base of each foot to create a seam that is perpendicular to the leg seam. This creates a toe and heel for your beastie.

Making the Head

1 Align the long sides of the head (A) pieces. (If you're using a fabric other than felt, the right sides should be touching.) Pin the pieces together all around the edges.

2 Leaving a ¼-inch (6 mm) seam allowance, backstitch along one pinned edge. (You'll just sew this one side together for now.)

3 Align the body with the head so that the head seam lines up with the torso seams. (Right sides should be touching.) Pin the pieces together.

4 Leaving a ¼-inch (6 mm) seam allowance, backstitch along the neck, from one edge of the jaw to the other. Leave the jaw area unstitched. (You'll attach the mouth there in the next step.)

Making the Zipper Mouth

1 Center the mouth (B) piece in the opening between the head and the front body. (If you're using a fabric other than felt, right sides should be together.)

2 Sandwich the zipper's tape (the fabric part) between the mouth, head, and body pieces. (The zipper's pull tab and slider should be inside the monster's mouth. If you're using fabrics other than felt, these parts are touching right sides of fabric.) Pin all the pieces together along the edges.

3 Leaving a ¼-inch (6 mm) seam allowance, backstitch along the pinned edge.

4 If you have not already done so, remove all the pins. Notch the fabric at the curves and corners.

Finishing Xipp It

1 Carefully turn the creature right side out. Stuff it as firmly as you want. Sew the opening closed.

2 Use the fabric pen to mark a spot on each side of the head, centered between the head seams and 2 inches (5 cm) above the upper zipper lip. Sew on two button eyes.

Xipp It doesn't mean to take unwelcome bites. Help Xipp behave by feeding it marbles or coins. Xipp its mouth shut when pets or small children visit.

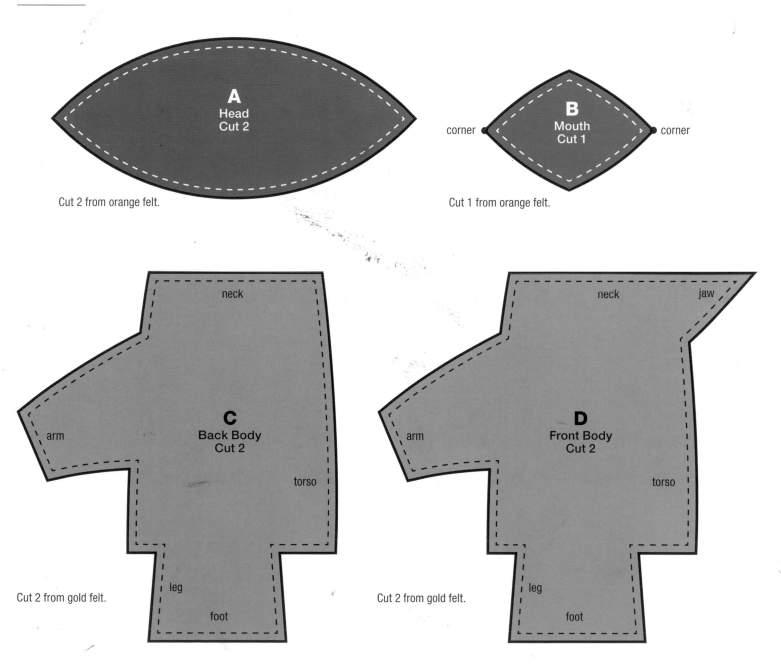

A
Head
Cut 2

Cut 2 from orange felt.

B
Mouth
Cut 1

corner

corner

Cut 1 from orange felt.

neck

C
Back Body
Cut 2

arm

torso

Cut 2 from gold felt.

leg

foot

neck

jaw

D
Front Body
Cut 2

arm

torso

Cut 2 from gold felt.

leg

foot

53

Floppyzoid Galaxy Discovered

Visits to its habitat will boost space tourism, say industry insiders

You Will Need

- Patterns (page 57)
- Basic Beastie Kit (page 8)
- Orange fleece, 7 x 11 inches (17.8 x 27.9 cm)
- Pink fleece, 7 x 7 inches (17.8 x 17.8 cm)
- White fleece, 7 x 4 inches (17.8 x 10.2 cm)
- Fuchsia fleece, 7 x 17 inches (17.8 x 43.2 cm)
- Green fleece, 19 x 13 inches (48.3 x 33 cm)
- Turquoise fleece, 7 x 8 inches (17.8 x 20.3 cm)
- Two 40 mm googly eyes or a pair of child-safe doll eyes
- Pellet-style synthetic stuffing (You need only a few spoonfuls, so buy the smallest amount available.)
- Spoon
- Hot-glue gun and glue sticks (follow manufacturer's directions for use)

Use the fabrics and colors noted on the patterns and the supplies list, or use whatever fabrics you like.

Making and Using Templates

1 Use the patterns to create the templates. Trace and cut your pieces, cutting each shape from the wrong side of the fabrics. For the arm (**F**) pieces, cut two pieces, then flip the template and cut the two remaining pieces. Set all the pieces aside.

This puppet-creature's floppy arms are one of a kind. (Well, okay, there are two of them.)

Making the Arms

1 Align each pair of arm (**F**) pieces, right sides together. Pin them together.

2 Leaving a ⅜-inch (9.5 mm) seam allowance, backstitch along the edges, leaving the shoulders open.

3 Notch at each angle of the wrist and between the thumb and the rest of the hand. Carefully turn the arm and hand inside out.

4 Pour a spoonful of pellet-style synthetic stuffing into the arm and work it down toward the hand. This will make the arm floppy. Repeat with the other arm. Set the arms aside.

Making the Tongue

1 Align the tongue (**A**) pieces rights sides together. Pin them together.

2 Leaving a ⅜-inch (9.5 mm) seam allowance, backstitch around the edge, leaving the straight end open.

3 Turn the tongue right side out. Starting at the open end, make a stitch down the middle of the tongue. Stop stitching ½ inch (1.3 cm) from the tip of the tongue. Then turn around at the end and stitch back up to the beginning, following the same line. (The loose ends of the stitch get sewn into the mouth seam later.)

4 Pour a spoonful of pellet-style synthetic stuffing inside the tongue, shoving equal amounts of pellets down either side of the center stitch. Set the tongue aside.

There's a bit more work to be done in Floppyzoid's maw. Good thing this beastie doesn't slobber.

Making the Mouth and Teeth

1 Align the straight edges of the two mouth (C) pieces, right sides together. Sandwich the tongue between them, centered, with its open edge aligned with the straight edges of the mouth pieces. Pin the pieces together.

2 Leaving a ⅜-inch (9.5 mm) seam allowance, backstitch across the straight side of the mouth and through the tongue.

3 Pin the teeth (D) pieces right sides together in pairs to form three teeth. Backstitch around the round edge of each tooth and leave the straight side open.

4 Turn each tooth right side out. Set the teeth aside.

Making the Head

1 Look at diagram 1 before reading this step. Align half of the mouth (as separated by the seam where the tongue is attached) with the circular head (E) piece, right sides together. Sandwich the teeth in between these two layers. Align the open edges of the teeth to match the round edges of the head and mouth. (See diagram 1.) Use pins wherever you need them.

2 Leaving ⅜-inch (9.5 mm) seam allowance, backstitch these aligned edges. Stitch through the teeth. This seam will be one half of a circle.

Making the Body

1 Align the rounded edge of the back body piece to the unstitched half of the head piece. (See diagram 2.) Pin these pieces together.

2 Leaving a ⅜-inch (9.5 mm) seam allowance, backstitch these edges together.

3 Align the unstitched half of the mouth with the rounded edge of the front body piece. (See diagram 3.) Pin these edges together.

4 Leaving a ⅜-inch (9.5 mm) seam allowance, backstitch these edges together.

5 Sandwich time. Align the unstitched, side edges of the body pieces together. Align the open edges of the arms with the side edges of the body about a ½ inch (1.3 cm) below the mouth seam. (See diagram 4.) Pin the pieces together.

6 Leaving a ⅜-inch (9.5 mm) seam allowance, backstitch from the corners of the mouth along the straight side of the body to the bottom. Repeat on the other side of the body. Leave the straight edge at the bottom open.

7 Want a hem on the bottom of your creature? (This will be on the straight edge where you'll insert your hand to use it as a puppet.) Fold up the bottom about ½ inch (1.3 cm) toward the right side of the body. Pin in place. Backstitch around on the edge of the fold. Or skip this step and go on to step 8.

8 If you haven't already, remove all the pins. Carefully, gently, turn Floppyzoid right side out. Attach the eyes using a hot-glue gun.

Stick your hand inside Floppyzoid and go on a tongue-wagging, arm-swinging rampage.

PATTERNS

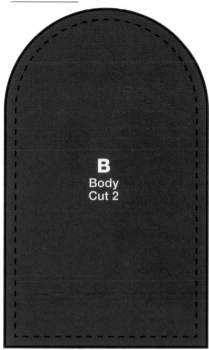

B
Body
Cut 2

Cut 1 from fuchsia fleece.
Cut 1 from orange fleece.

C
Mouth
Cut 2

Cut 2 from pink fleece.

E
Head
Cut 1

Cut 1 from fuchsia fleece.

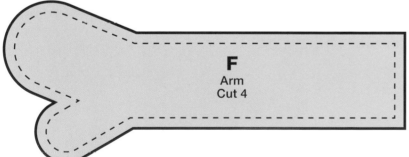

F
Arm
Cut 4

Cut 4 from green fleece.

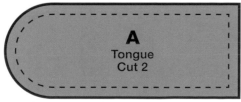

A
Tongue
Cut 2

Cut 2 from turquoise fleece.

D
Tooth
Cut 6

Cut 6 from
white fleece.

DIAGRAMS

1.

Head

Teeth, sewn
and turned

Mouth, assembled

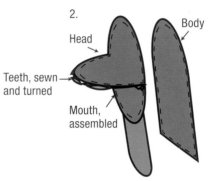

2.

Head

Body

Teeth, sewn
and turned

Mouth,
assembled

3.

Head

Teeth, sewn
and turned

Back of body

Mouth,
assembled

Front of body

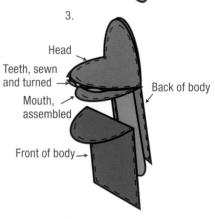

4.

Head

Teeth, sewn
and turned

Arm's open edge

Mouth,
assembled

Front of body

Back of body

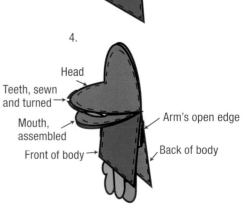

Terrifying Totebaggers Stage Full-Moon Foray

Toothy, four-eyed freaks frighten city residents

Totebaggers' Instructions

You Will Need

- Patterns (page 61)
- Basic Beastie Kit (page 8)
- Dark blue fleece, ½ yard (45.7 cm)
- Light blue fleece, ½ yard (45.7 cm)
- Red fleece, 12 x 12 inches (30.5 x 30.5 cm)
- 2 pairs of child-safe doll eyes

Use the fabrics and colors noted on the patterns and the supplies list, or use whatever fabrics you like.

Making and Using Templates

1. Use the patterns to create templates. Trace and cut your pieces from the wrong side of the fabrics. Set the pieces aside. For the arm (B) pieces, cut two pieces, and then flip the template. Cut the two remaining pieces. Set all the pieces aside.

Time for some dental work.

Making the Teeth and Mouth

1. Align the two teeth (D) pieces, right sides together. Backstitch the bumpy (toothy) edge together. Leave the straight edges open.

2. Notch the curves and corners. Turn the teeth right side out. Lightly stuff the teeth. Set them aside.

3. Center the mouth (F) over the opening in the front body (A). The wrong side of the mouth should be touching the right side of the front body. Sandwich the straight edge of the teeth between the mouth and body. Pin the edges.

4. Leaving a ¼-inch (6 mm) seam allowance, whipstitch the pieces together around the rim of the opening. (If using a sewing machine, use a zigzag stitch on all pieces.) This is now the inside edge of the mouth.

5. Whipstitch around the outer edges of the mouth. Set aside.

This beast likes to hang around.
So make it some arms!

Making the Arms

(1) Grab the four arm (**B**) pieces. Align them in matching pairs, right sides together. Pin each pair together.

(2) Leaving a ¼-inch (6 mm) seam allowance, backstitch the matched edges on each arm set. Leave the straight ends open.

(3) Notch the curve between the finger nubs on both hands. Turn each sewn arm right side out. Turn out the fingers, too.

(4) Overlap the fingers so that the arms form a semicircle. Stitch the hands together where the fingers overlap.

Making the Feet

(1) Grab a foot (**E**) piece. Fold it short end to short end, right sides together. Leaving a ¼-inch (6 mm) seam allowance, backstitch the short edges, leaving the long edge open.

(2) Repeat step 1 for the other foot piece.

(3) Turn each foot right side out. Set aside.

Don't keep this freak waiting.
It wants you to put it together.

Assembling the Creature

(1) Grab the back body (**C**) piece. Place it right side up. Sandwich the arms and feet between the back and front body pieces so the open edges align. (The arms and feet will be inside the sandwich. You'll need to fold the arms so they fit inside and don't get in the way of the seam you'll sew in step 2.)

(2) Pin the layers in place, pinning along the outside edges of the back body. Leaving a ¼-inch (6 mm) seam allowance, backstitch all the way around the body.

(3) If you haven't already done so, remove all the pins. Gently turn the creature right side out through its mouth.

So far, this creature is all mouth and teeth. Show everyone its sensitive side by adding eyes.

Attaching the Eyes

(1) Fold the top of the mouth up, toward the inside of Totebagger's body. Make a mark where you'd like each eye. (You can place them wherever you like.)

(2) On each mark, snip a small hole no wider than the shaft of the eye you'll insert there.

(3) Working from the right side of the body, insert an eye into an eyehole so that the shaft pokes through to the wrong side. Secure the washer on the shaft. Repeat this step for each remaining eyehole.

Your Totebagger is ready to serve you.
It wants to hug one of your
shoulders and carry your stuff.
You should let it!

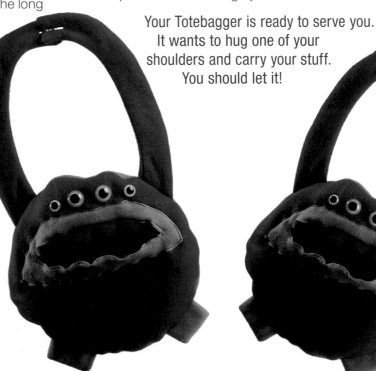

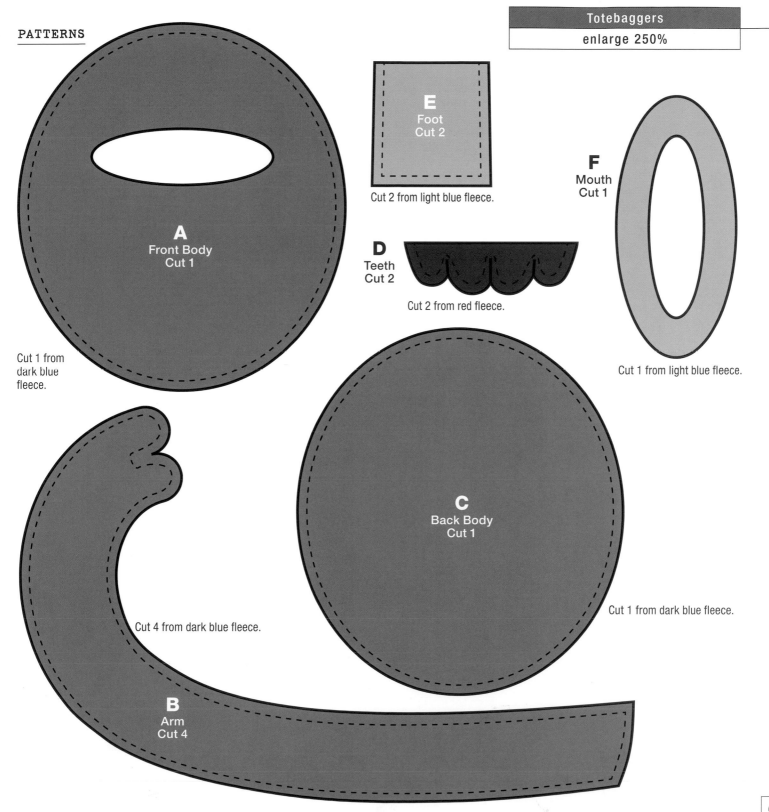

PATTERNS

Totebaggers
enlarge 250%

E
Foot
Cut 2

Cut 2 from light blue fleece.

F
Mouth
Cut 1

Cut 1 from light blue fleece.

A
Front Body
Cut 1

Cut 1 from
dark blue
fleece.

D
Teeth
Cut 2

Cut 2 from red fleece.

C
Back Body
Cut 1

Cut 1 from dark blue fleece.

Cut 4 from dark blue fleece.

B
Arm
Cut 4

Factory Produces Creepers of the Door

Revelation fuels debate on the dangers of genetic engineering

You Will Need

- Patterns (pages 66-67)
- Basic Beastie Kit (page 8)
- Faux fur, ¼ yard (22.9 cm), for each creature
- Cotton fabric, ¼ yard (22.9 cm), for each creature
- Fleece in 3 colors, ¼ yard (22.9 cm) of each color, for each creature
- Fleece, 3 x 4 inches (7.6 cm x 10.2 cm), for each creature
- Swatch of white felt, 8 x 16 inches (20.3 x 40.6 cm), for Guardian Creeper
- White felt scraps for Attack Creeper's teeth
- 3 to 4 child-safe doll eyes for each creature
- 1 necktie for each Creeper

A sewing machine is highly recommended for this project.

Use the fabrics and colors noted on the patterns and the supplies list, or use whatever fabrics you like.

Making and Using Templates

1 Decide which Creeper to make. Either will be happy to guard your door, taking messages for you or sending a message—do not disturb! Use the patterns to create templates. Trace and cut your pieces from the wrong side of the fabrics. Making a Creeper with eyelids or teeth? Read step 2.

2 For the eyelid (I) pieces on the Guardian Creeper's side, cut one piece, and then flip the template and cut the remaining piece.

3 For the teeth on the Attack Creeper's Do Not Disturb side, draw as many triangles as you would like directly on white felt. The triangles should be no smaller than 1 inch (2.5 cm) long and ½ inch (1.3 cm) wide at the base. Cut them out. Set all the pieces aside.

Making Arms and a Tongue

1 Align the right sides of a pair of arm (E) pieces. (Each side should be a different color.) Pin each pair together. Leaving a ¼-inch (6 mm) seam allowance, backstitch the pieces together. Leave the straight ends open. Repeat for the other arm. If you're making a tongue, repeat using the tongue (J) pieces.

2 Notch the curves. Then gently turn each arm inside out. Stuff it lightly. Turn the tongue inside out. Don't stuff it. Instead, backstitch a seam from one short end to the other. Set all the parts aside.

Assembling the Do Not Disturb Side

1 Grab your Do Not Disturb side pieces: the body (F), face appliqué (G), legs appliqué (H), eyelid (I) or eye base patch (I), and tongue (J), or teeth pieces.

2 Align the face and legs pieces atop the body piece, right sides up. Pin the top of the face to the top of the head and the lower part of the legs to the lower part of the body.

3 Lift the face up just enough to position the eyelid or eye pad pieces right side up atop the body piece. (See the finished Creepers for placement ideas.) Then lay the face back down. The eye pieces should be held in place by the face. You can pin them if you like.

4 To place the upper teeth, lift up the lower end of the face just enough to arrange teeth so the lower edge of the face overlaps the teeth by about ¼ inch (6 mm). Then lay the face back down. Pin in place if you like. Use the appliqué technique (page 13) to secure the face appliqué and teeth to the body. Leave the bottoms of the teeth loose.

5 To place the lower teeth and the tongue, lift up the top of the legs appliqué just enough to arrange the teeth and tongue. Then lay the legs piece back down. Pin in place if you like. Appliqué along its top edge to secure the teeth and tongue. Leave the tops of the teeth and end of the tongue loose.

6 Finally, appliqué the face's eye openings to secure the eyelids or eye pad in place. You should have appliquéd everything to the body by stitching along all edges. (You'll sew seams all around the sides of the body later, to attach arms and necktie hangers when you assemble your Creeper.)

You're almost finished with one of your Creeper's faces. All that's left are the eyes.

Do Not Disturb
Attack Creeper

Leave a Message
Attack Creeper

Making the Eyes (Do Not Disturb side)

1 Turn the Do Not Disturb side of the body right side up. Use the fabric pen to make a mark in the front center of the eye pad(s) where you want the eye to go. (On Guardian Creeper, it may seem as if your mark is too close to the eyelid. It's not—each eyelid is supposed to cover its eye a little bit.)

2 On each mark, snip a small hole no wider than the shaft of the eye you'll insert there. Cut through both the eye pad and the body piece.

3 Insert an eye into an eyehole so that the shaft pokes through to the wrong side of the creature. Secure the washer on the shaft. Repeat this step for each remaining eyehole.

Enough of this Do Not Disturb side. Turn to the friendly Leave a Message side of your Creeper.

Making the Pocket

1 Both Creepers have a pocket. Align the pocket lining (D) and pocket (D) pieces with right sides touching. Leaving a ¼-inch (6 mm) seam allowance, backstitch along the straight top edge of the pieces.

2 Flip the pocket, hiding the seam. Smooth the pocket and align its bottom edges. Then align the bottom of the pocket with the Leave a Message body (A) piece. Pin these together. Set them aside.

Making the Lips

1 Both Creepers have lips. Fold the lip (C) piece in half, from long edge to long edge. Be sure the right side of the fabric is on the outside. Backstitch the long edges together, leaving a ¼-inch (6 mm) seam allowance. You should have a long fleece tube. Set the tube aside.

You've made the pocket and the lips. Put it all together.

Assembling the Leave a Message Side

1 Make sure your Leave a Message side body (**A**) is right side up. Align the eye pad (**B**) piece(s), right side up, underneath the eyeholes. Backstitch or zigzag stitch the edges of the eyeholes to secure the eye pad piece(s).

2 Turn the lip tube you made earlier right side out. Lay this tube horizontally atop the right side of the Leave a Message body (**A**) piece, at least 2½ inches (5 cm) from the top of the body.

3 Backstitch horizontally through the middle of the lip tube to attach it to the body.

4 Add eyes to this side of the creature using the earlier directions for Making the Eyes. Locate the eye pads on the top half of the body to leave plenty of room for the lip to be appliquéd below. Set the creature aside.

Creeper Sandwich Time

1 Place the Do Not Disturb side of your Creeper right side up. Grab the arms with the sides matching the Do Not Disturb side and lay those sides down on the body. Align the open edges of the arms with the outer edge of the Creeper so they overlap to create a ¼-inch (6 mm) seam allowance. Pin in place.

2 Trim a necktie to a length that will make a suitable loop for fitting easily around a doorknob. Align each of the two trimmed ends of the necktie with the top the body. The loop of the necktie should overlap the body, with the top of the loop pointing toward the feet so that it can be sandwiched inside.

3 Lay the Leave a Message side of your Creeper right side down atop the necktie, arms, and Do Not Disturb side of the creature. Here's your Creeper sandwich. Pin together.

4 Beginning at the inside of one of the legs, backstitch all the way around the outside edge, leaving at a ¼-inch (6 mm) seam allowance. Leave a 2-inch (5 cm) opening between the legs for stuffing.

5 Remove all the pins. Gently turn your Creeper right side out. Stuff the Creeper as firmly as you want. Sew the stuffing hole closed.

Hang the Creeper on your door to fend off invaders or invite correspondence.

Do Not Disturb
Guardian Creeper

Leave a Message
Guardian Creeper

PATTERNS

A
Body
"Leave a Message"
side
Cut 1

Cut 1 from yellow fleece.

B
Eye Pad
Cut 2

Cut 2 from
maroon
fleece.

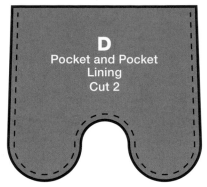

D
Pocket and Pocket
Lining
Cut 2

Cut 1 from multicolor faux fur.
Cut 1 from cotton.

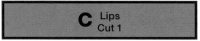

C Lips
Cut 1

Cut 1 from orange fleece.

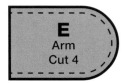

E
Arm
Cut 4

Cut 2 from yellow fleece.
Cut 2 from orange fleece.

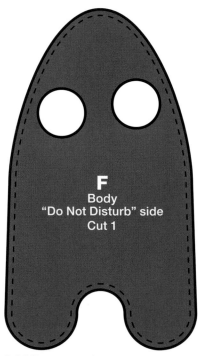

F
Body
"Do Not Disturb" side
Cut 1

Cut 1 from maroon fleece.

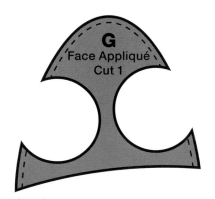

G
Face Appliqué
Cut 1

Cut 1 from orange fleece.

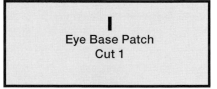

I
Eye Base Patch
Cut 1

Cut 1 from yellow fleece.

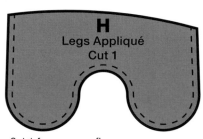

H
Legs Appliqué
Cut 1

Cut 1 from orange fleece.

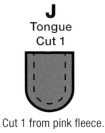

J
Tongue
Cut 1

Cut 1 from pink fleece.

PATTERNS

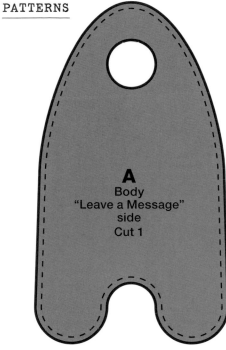

A
Body
"Leave a Message"
side
Cut 1

Cut 1 from pink fleece.

B
Eye Pad
Cut 1

Cut 1 from
green faux
fur.

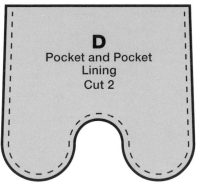

D
Pocket and Pocket
Lining
Cut 2

Cut 1 from green faux fur.
Cut 1 from cotton.

C Lips
Cut 1

Cut 1 from orange fleece.

E
Arm
Cut 4

Cut 2 from pink fleece.
Cut 2 from maroon fleece.

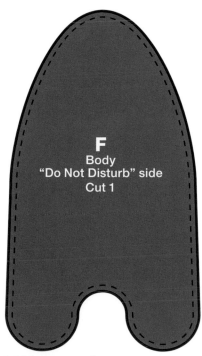

F
Body
"Do Not Disturb" side
Cut 1

Cut 1 from maroon fleece.

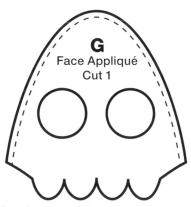

G
Face Appliqué
Cut 1

Cut 1 from white felt.

I
Eyelid
Cut 2

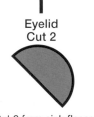

Cut 2 from pink fleece.

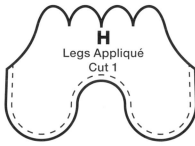

H
Legs Appliqué
Cut 1

Cut 1 from white felt.

Thingtones Spark Cell Phone Riots

Thingtone's Instructions

You Will Need

- Patterns (pages 72-73)
- Basic Beastie Kit (page 8)
- Orange or blue faux fur, 8 x 8 inches (20.3 x 20.3 cm), per creature
- White felt for teeth, 1 x 1 inch (2.5 x 2.5 cm), per creature
- Yellow or orange fleece, 3 x 3 inches (7.6 x 7.6 cm), per creature
- Green or yellow fleece, 3 x 3 inches (7.6 x 7.6 cm), per creature
- Lightweight printed or paisley cotton fabric, 8 x 8 inches (20.3 x 20.3 cm), per creature
- 2 pairs of buttons or 1 pair of child-safe doll eyes for each creature
- Hook-and-loop tape

A sewing machine is strongly recommended for this project.

Use the fabrics and colors noted on the patterns and the supplies list, or use whatever you like.

Making the Patterns and Parts

1 First, you're going to measure your cell phone so that it will fit inside the Thingtone you make. Close the phone (if it opens). Wrap your measuring tape all the way around its middle. Write down the number and add ½ inch (1.3 cm) for seam allowance. Divide the new number by 2. (If you have stray eighths or sixteenths of inches, round up to the next ¼ inch [6 mm].) This number is the width of your Thingtone.

2 Measure the height of the phone. Write down the number and add ½ inch (1.3 cm) for seam allowance. This number is the depth of your creature's pocket.

3 On card stock, draw a rectangle that is the same width and height as the measurements you just determined. This is the template for the interior lining (A). Trace and cut it from lightweight printed cotton. Set aside.

4 Now make the template for the tummy (B), the outside front of the Thingtone. Add ½ inch (1.3 cm) to the length of the interior lining template you made in step 3. On card stock, draw a new rectangle using those measurements. Then draw a horizontal line 2 inches (5 cm) down from one

of the short ends of this rectangle. This creates a rectangle that is 2 inches (5 cm) tall. Cut off that small rectangle and use it as the template for the face (C). The remaining rectangle is the tummy (B) template.

5 Trace and cut the face template from the wrong side of the fleece. Set the cut piece aside.

6 Trace and cut the tummy template from the wrong side of the faux fur. Set the cut piece aside.

7 Trace and cut the arms (H) pieces from the wrong side of the fleece. Set the pieces aside.

No self-respecting Thingtone would ever drop the phone. So this creature needs a tab closure to keep the phone securely in its belly.

Making the Tab Closure

1 Measure the thickness of your phone. Write down the number and add 2 inches (5 cm) to it. This is the length of the close tab (D and E) pieces. The width of the close tab should be 1¾ inches (4.4 cm).

2 Draw a rectangle using these measurements. Draw rounded corners on one end. Trace and cut the template twice, once from the cotton lining fabric (for E) and once from the fleece (for D). Set the tab aside.

How's the Thingtone going to tell you who called without a mouth? And how will it latch to you?

Making the Lip, Teeth, and Loops

1 Earlier you wrote down the measurement from the interior lining (A) template. (See step 3 of Making the Patterns and Parts.) Draw another rectangle the same width and 1½ inches (3.8 cm) tall. This is the template for the lip. (F) Trace and cut it from the green or yellow fleece.

2 Trace and cut the tooth (G) pieces from the white felt. Make as many as you want.

3 Decide if you want one loop or two to hang Thingtone from your belt. Make the loops using the Handy Hang Tab Instructions on pages 20-21.

There's a Thingtone holding for you on Line 1. It would like for you to put its face together now.

Face Sandwich

1 Put the teeth on top of the tummy with their top edges touching the top (right side up) edge of the faux fur. (See diagram 1.)

2 Fold the lip in half, right side out, so it's ¾ inches (1.9 cm) tall. (See diagram 2.) Place the lip, with the fold pointing downward, atop the tummy and teeth. Align the open edge of the lip with the top edge of the tummy. (See diagram 3.)

3 Align the face, right side down, with the top edge of the tummy. The lips and teeth will be sandwiched between the faux fur and the face. Carefully pin this mass of layers together. (See diagram 4.)

4 If you have a sewing machine, you'll want to use it now. Backstitch the edges together, leaving a ¼-inch (6 mm) seam allowance. (See diagram 5.)

Keep Tabs on Your Phone

1 Grab the tab closure (**D** and **E**) pieces. Pin them right sides together. Backstitch from the straight, narrow end down the length of the tab, around the curve, and back up the other side. Leave the straight, narrow end open.

2 Notch the curve and turn the tab right side out. Smooth out the seam allowance that might be bunching up inside. Finish stitching around the edge of the tab, about ⅛ inch (3 mm) in, to close the end.

Don't forget to give your Thingtone arms!

Assembling Arms

1 Pin two arm (**H**) pieces, right sides together. Starting at one side of the narrow, straight edge stitch around the arm to the other straight edge. Leave the edge open.

2 Notch the curve. Repeat step 1 to make the other arm.

Now it's time to give your Thingtone some insides.

Attaching the Front and Lining

1 Place the interior lining right side up. Center the tab closure, lining side down, on top of the interior lining. Align the straight, narrow edge of the tab with the bottom edge of the interior lining.

2 Place the hang tab loop or loops atop the tab, or on either side of the tab closure. The fold of each loop must point downward. Align the ends of each loop with the edge of the interior lining.

3 Place the faux fur body right side down atop the interior lining. The tummy should be touching the bottom edge with the tabs and loops. Align all the edges and pin them in place.

4 Backstitch the short edges of the lining and the front body where they match. Do not stitch the long edges yet.

5 Turn the body right side out and smooth it flat. The faux fur side should be facing up.

Your Thingtone is almost done....

Attaching the Arms

1 Place the arms atop the faux fur, just below the face. Align the narrow, straight edges of the arms with the edges of the body.

2 Fold the body so that the front and back are touching, wrong sides in. Place the straight edges of the arms between the layers of the body. (The tab and loop should be hanging out.) Align the edges and pin the sides of the body and the arm edges together.

3 Carefully backstitch down both sides of the body, leaving a ⅜-inch (9.5 mm) seam allowance. Sewing through this many layers of fabric can be tricky, so make sure you keep the edges aligned, and use a sewing machine if you can.

4 To bind the raw edges of the body fabric, whipstitch by hand or use the sewing machine to zigzag stitch down the sides of the body. This stitch will go between the edges of the fabric and the seam you made in step 3.

No, really. This time it IS almost done.

Finishing Touches

1 Cut a piece of hook-and-loop tape slightly smaller than the end of the close tab. Make sure you have a piece of the hook side and the loop side of the tape.

2 Put your phone inside the Thingtone. Close the close tab. Mark where the end of the close tab hits the face.

3 Backstitch one side of the hook-and-loop tape to the underside of the close tab. Backstitch the other side to just about the same spot you marked on the face. The sides of the hook-and-loop tape should match up when you close the phone.

4 Sew the eye or eyes to the face or the tab.

Slip the loops onto your belt. Your Thingtone is ready to keep track of your phone. A word of warning: Do not let your Thingtone phone home. Intergalactic cell phone charges are astronomical.

PATTERNS

A
Interior lining
Cut 1

Cut 1 from printed cotton.

You will use your phone to determine the dimensions of this pattern. See the instructions.

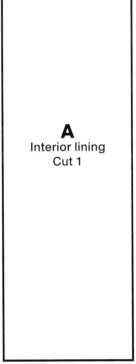

B
Tummy
Cut 1

Cut 1 from faux fur.

You will use your phone to determine the dimensions of this pattern. See the instructions.

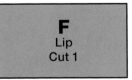

C
Face
Cut 1

Cut 1 from fleece.

You will use your phone to determine the dimensions of this pattern. See the instructions.

F
Lip
Cut 1

Cut 1 from fleece.

You will use your phone to determine the dimensions of this pattern. See the instructions.

D
Close tab, outside
Cut 1

Cut 1 from fleece.

You will use your phone to determine the dimensions of this pattern. See the instructions.

E
Close tab, lining
Cut 1

Cut 1 from printed cotton.

You will use your phone to determine the dimensions of this pattern. See the instructions.

G
Tooth
Cut 2

Cut 2 from white felt.

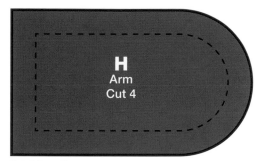

H
Arm
Cut 4

Cut 4 from fleece.

DIAGRAMS

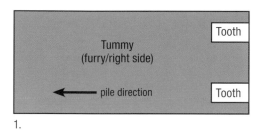

Tummy (furry/right side)

Tooth

Tooth

← pile direction

1.

Lip

Fold it in half.

2.

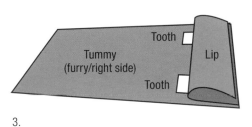

Tummy (furry/right side)

Tooth

Tooth

Lip

3.

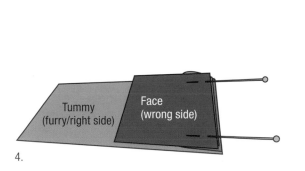

Tummy (furry/right side)

Face (wrong side)

4.

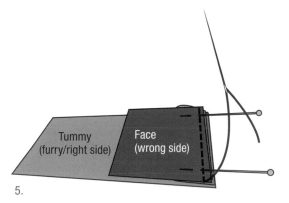

Tummy (furry/right side)

Face (wrong side)

5.

Did Pursival Plushies Build Stonehenge?

Purse-like creatures reveal similar prehistoric monument on home planet

You Will Need

- Patterns (pages 78-79)
- Basic Beastie Kit (page 8)
- Green or pink faux fur, ½ yard (45.7 cm), for each creature
- Pink or orange fleece, two 8 x 1½-inch (20.3 x 3.8 cm) pieces, for each creature
- Orange or maroon fleece, ¼ yard (22.9 cm), for each creature
- Striped fleece, ¼ yard (22.9 cm), for optional variation on ears and arms
- Lightweight cotton, ½ yard (45.7 cm), for each creature
- Necktie for each creature
- Zipper for each creature (optional), 7 inches (17.8 cm)
- 2 child-safe doll eyes for each creature

A sewing machine is strongly recommended to make these plushies.

Use the fabrics and colors noted on the patterns and the supplies list, or use whatever fabrics you like.

Making and Using Templates

1 Which Pursival will you make first—one with ears or one without? Use the patterns to create the templates you'll need. Trace and cut your pieces from the wrong side of the fabrics. For the ear (G) pieces, cut two pieces and then flip the template before cutting the other two pieces. Set all the pieces aside.

Preparing the Pursivals' Parts

1 Match a pair of arm/leg (D) pieces, rights sides together. If you are using striped fleece, make sure the stripes line up along the seams. Leaving a ¼-inch (6 mm) seam allowance, backstitch the pieces together, leaving the straight edge open. (The straight edge is where the arm or leg will attach to the body.) Repeat for the remaining arm and leg pieces. If you aren't making ears, skip to step 4.

2 If you're making ears, first you need to make the strap that will attach to them. Take the necktie and snip off the point on its wide end. Fold the tie in half to gauge what length you want Pursival's strap to be. Cut it from either end to make it the length you want.

3 Now match a pair of ear (G) pieces, right sides together. Slip one end of the tie between the front and the back of the ear pieces. Match the edge of the tie to the bottom edge of the ear. Leaving a ¼-inch (6 mm) seam allowance, backstitch the pieces together, leaving the straight edge open. (The straight edge is where the ear will attach to the body.) Repeat for the remaining pair of ear pieces. Make sure the tie is not twisted before you attach it to the second ear.

4 Notch any curves or corners. Flip each arm, leg, and ear right side out. Lightly stuff them. Set aside.

5 Reinforce the ears by stitching around the outer edge, leaving a ¼-inch (6 mm) seam allowance. At the top edge of each ear, catch the tie in the seam.

Your Pursival can pucker up—if you give it lips.

Fish Mouth

Making the Lips

(1) Grab the front body lining (C) and place it right side up in front of you. Fold one of the lip (B) pieces in half, from long edge to long edge. Make sure the right side of the fabric is on the outside. Match the long, open edge of the folded lip to the straight edge of the body lining.

(2) Place the front body (C) right side down atop of the front body lining and lip. Match the straight edges. Pin together. Leaving a ¼-inch (6 mm) seam allowance, backstitch all the layers together along the straight edge. The lower lip is done.

(3) Are you making the earless Pursival? Snip off the point of the necktie on its wide end. Fold the tie in half, short end to short end, to gauge what length you want the Pursival's strap to be. Cut it from either end to the length you want.

(4) Grab the head (A) piece and place it right side up in front of you. For the earless Pursival, line up the wide edge of the necktie with the straight edge of the head piece. Take the other lip (B) piece and fold it as you did in step 1.

(5) Match the long, open edge of the folded lip to the straight edge of the head. Place the head lining (A) face-down atop the lip, tie (only if your Pursival is earless!), and head. Match the straight edges. Pin together. Leaving a ¼-inch (6 mm) seam allowance, backstitch all the layers together along the straight edge.

(6) Flip both the head and the body right side out so that the seam is hidden. Smooth the layers and match up their edges.

If you really want to keep this monster's mouth shut, install a zipper.

Zipper Option

(1) Putting a zipper in the Pursival's mouth? Use the zipper instructions for Xipp It on page 52. Sandwich the zipper in between the lips you made and the head lining (A) and body lining (C) pieces.

Attaching the Eyes

(1) On the head lining (A) piece, make a mark where you'd like each eye. On each mark, snip a small hole no wider than the shaft of the eye you'll insert there. It's easiest to cut from the lining side.

(2) Working from the right side of the body, insert an eye into an eyehole so that the shaft pokes through to the wrong side. Repeat for each eye. If you're making the earless Pursival, snip holes in the tie so the eyes can clamp the necktie in place. (See how the finished Pursival has two eyes that hold the tie in place just above its mouth.)

(3) Secure the washer on the shaft of each eye. Set the whole front body aside.

A Pursival's hairy chest conceals a secret pocket. Make it now.

Making the Pocket

1 Align the pocket lining (**F**) piece and the pocket (**F**) piece with right sides together. Pin the curved edges together. Leaving a ¼-seam (6 mm) allowance, backstitch them together. Leave a 2-inch (5 cm) opening so you can turn the pocket right side out.

2 If you haven't done so already, remove the pins. Notch any curves. Flip the pocket right side out. Smooth the panels. Set this piece aside.

Assembling the Pursival

1 You'll put everything you've made together in a sandwich. Begin by placing the back lining (**E**) piece right side down. Align the back (**E**) piece right side up atop the lining. Pin the edges together.

2 Time for the next layer. If you made ears, lay them atop the right-side-up back piece. Align the open edges of the ears with the edge of the back, with ¼-inch (6 mm) overhang for the seam allowance. Pin the ears in place.

3 If you didn't make ears, go ahead and add the other end of the tie to the Pursival. Line up the free edge of the tie with the top of the head (**A**), with a ¼-inch (6 mm) overhang for the seam allowance. Make sure the tie is not twisted. Place the rest of the tie inside the Pursival's body, well away from where you will sew the seams. Pin the tie in place.

4 Your sandwich is getting thick. That's why a sewing machine is recommended. Time to add another layer: place the head, eyes down, atop the sandwich. Pin its edges. Leaving a ¼-inch (6 mm) seam allowance, backstitch along the edges of the head.

5 Now you can add the arms and legs. Align the open edges of each arm and leg with the outer edge of the back body (**E**). Make sure the rounded edges of the arms and feet are pointing inward. Two more layers and you're done stacking.

Zipper Mouth

6 Place the Pursival's pocket, fur side down and lining side up, on top of its right-side-up back piece. Match the rounded edges. Make sure the tie (which is tucked inside the Pursival's body right now) is well away from the edges.

7 Time for the final layer! Place the Pursival's front body, fleece side down, atop the pocket and back. Match the curved edges and make sure the lips overlap. Pin all the layers together.

8 Leaving a ¼-inch (6 mm) seam allowance, whipstitch or zigzag the layers together.

9 Remove all the pins. Carefully turn your Pursival right side out.

Sling your Pursival over your shoulder and fill its guts with whatever you want. Maybe a guidebook for touring ancient ruins, or a map of space?

PATTERNS

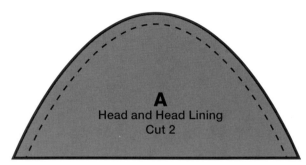

A
Head and Head Lining
Cut 2

Cut 1 from orange or maroon fleece.
Cut 1 from lightweight cotton.

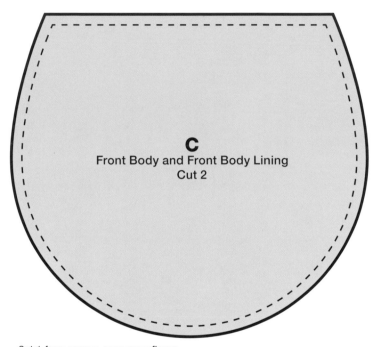

C
Front Body and Front Body Lining
Cut 2

Cut 1 from orange or maroon fleece.
Cut 1 from lightweight cotton.

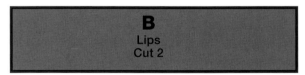

B
Lips
Cut 2

Cut 2 from pink or orange fleece.

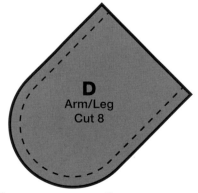

D
Arm/Leg
Cut 8

Cut 8 from orange or maroon fleece.

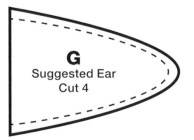

G
Suggested Ear
Cut 4

Cut 4 from striped fleece.

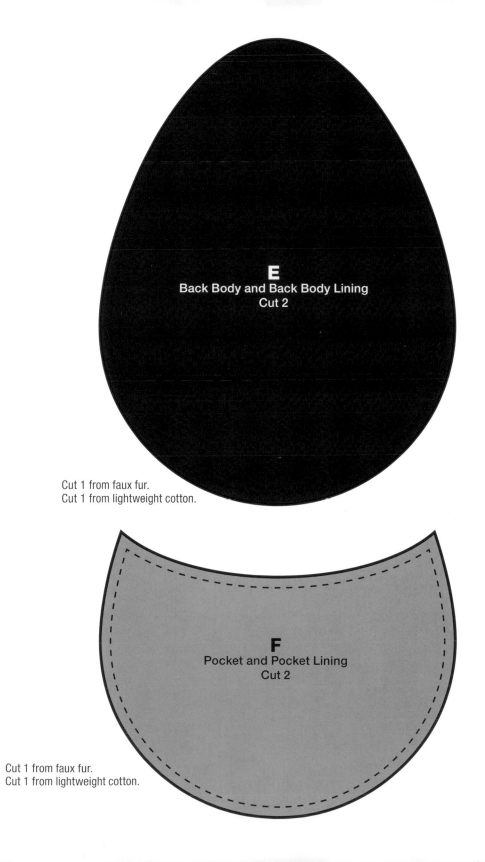

E
Back Body and Back Body Lining
Cut 2

Cut 1 from faux fur.
Cut 1 from lightweight cotton.

F
Pocket and Pocket Lining
Cut 2

Cut 1 from faux fur.
Cut 1 from lightweight cotton.

Feeteaters Disrupt Barefoot Convention

Dread gives way to delight; cozy toes reported

You Will Need

- Patterns (page 83)
- Basic Beastie Kit (page 8)
- Old wool sweater for felting or felt, ½ yard (45.7 cm) (Use sweaters in two different colors if you want contrasting feet bottoms.)
- Washing machine, detergent, and dryer, or sink and laundry detergent (optional, if felting a sweater)
- Black felt, 2 x 2 inches (5 x 5 cm)
- White felt, 2 x 2 inches (5 x 5 cm)
- Red felt, 2 x 2 inches (5 x 5 cm)
- Polyester thread in black and white
- Polyester thread in the same color as the sweater
- 2 pom-poms
- Hot-glue gun and glue sticks (follow manufacturer's directions for use)

Use the fabrics and colors noted on the patterns and the supplies list, or use whatever fabrics you like.

Felting Your Sweater

1. Turn your wool sweater into felt. Here's how: wash it in a washing machine at the hottest water setting. Be sure to add detergent. After washing, the fabric should be shrunken and dense. It has become felt.

2. Put it in a clothes dryer on the hottest setting. It should become even denser and make super snuggly Feeteaters.

3. To work by hand, place the sweater in a sink filled with very warm water and a dash of laundry detergent. Swish the sweater with your hands until the fibers begin to meld. This may take 15 minutes or more of work, but it's fun because you can see and feel the felting action occur. Felting is completed when you can hardly make out the individual stitches of the sweater anymore. Then wring the water out of the sweater. Dry the sweater in the dryer.

Making and Using Templates

1 The patterns labeled **A** and **B** are guides for what the bottoms and sides of your slippers should look like. You'll need to do some measuring to get the correct dimensions for your feet to adjust the patterns. Grab a piece of paper. Step on it with one of your bare feet. Use a pencil to trace around your foot. This will be one of your bottom (**A**) patterns. Repeat this step with your other foot. Label each bottom (**A**) pattern right or left.

2 Measure the length of one of your bottom (**A**) patterns. Draw a side (**B**) piece to that length. Repeat until you've drawn a total of four side (**B**) pieces (two for each foot).

3 Use these patterns you've made plus the mouth (**C**), eyeball (**D**), pupil (**E**), and tooth (**F**) patterns to create templates. Then trace and cut out each shape from the felt.

Making Feeteaters

1 Pin together a pair of side panel pieces (**B**) at the front. Repeat for the second pair of side panel pieces.

2 Using a zigzag stitch, sew along the pinned edges so the stitches are on the outside edge of the fabric. There's no seam allowance.

3 Arrange the face pieces (**C**, **D**, **E**, and **F**) on the toes of the slipper. (See the photos of the finished Feeteaters for guidance.) Pin in place. Using a thread color you like (this thread will be seen on the outside of your Feeteater), zigzag stitch to sew the mouth, tooth, eyeball, and pupil pieces in place.

4 Pin together the top and back of the two side panels. Backstitch together right along the edges. Reinforce each seam at the ends by doing a few extra stitches on top of the seam.

5 Match a bottom (**A**) piece to one pair of side panels. Align the middle of the wide front to the front seam and the middle of the heel to the back seam. Repeat this step for the other bottom (**A**) piece.

6 Backstitch along the pinned edges of each slipper so the stitches are on the outside edge of the fabric. Remove all the pins.

7 Hot glue a pom-pom on each nose.

Slip these creatures on your toes.
They won't actually EAT your feet. (Will they?)

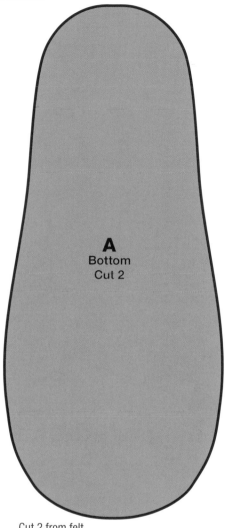

A
Bottom
Cut 2

Cut 2 from felt.

You will use your feet to determine the dimensions of this pattern. See the instructions.

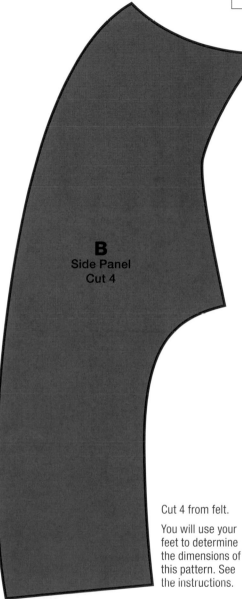

B
Side Panel
Cut 4

Cut 4 from felt.

You will use your feet to determine the dimensions of this pattern. See the instructions.

D
Eyeball
Cut 4

Cut 4 from white felt.

E
Pupil
Cut 4

Cut 4 from black felt.

F
Tooth
Cut 8

Cut 8 from white felt.

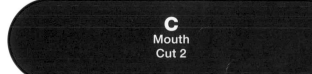

C
Mouth
Cut 2

Cut 2 from red felt.

Nauseators Overwhelm Air Traffic Controllers

Plush helmets rule the skies; are they friendly or fearsome?

You Will Need

- Patterns (page 88)
- Basic Beastie Kit (page 8)
- Blue or pink faux fur, ½ yard (45.7 cm), for each creature
- Green faux fur, ½ yard (45.7 cm), for each creature
- White felt, 1½ x 2 inches (3.8 x 5 cm), for each creature
- Red or orange fleece, ½ yard (45.7 cm), for each creature
- Red fleece and printed cotton, ½ yard (45.7 cm), for each creature
- Hook-and-loop tape
- 1 or 2 pairs of child-safe doll eyes or cat eyes for each creature

Use the fabrics and colors noted on the patterns and the supplies list, or use whatever fabrics you like.

Making and Using Templates

1. Use the patterns to create templates. Trace and cut your pieces from the wrong side of the fabrics. For the side panels (A), cut one piece from each fabric suggested, and then flip the template before cutting the second piece from each fabric. Set all the pieces aside.

2. If you want your Nauseator to have horns (G) or ears (H), use the correct patterns to create those templates. Then trace and cut out the appendages, flipping the templates to cut the second pieces from the suggested fabrics.

Making the Horns or Ears

1. To make the horns (G), align the pieces as matched pairs, right sides together. Pin them in place.

2. Backstitch each horn from one side of the flat, narrow edge, around the top, to the other side. Notch the curve. Turn the horn right side out.

3 Repeat steps 1 and 2 to make the second horn. Set the horns aside.

4 To make ears (H), align the pieces as matched pairs, right sides together. Pin them in place.

5 Backstitch each ear from one side of the flat, narrow edge, around the top, to the other side, leaving the end open. Notch the curve.

6 If you want, add the eyelid (F) and eye to the fleece part of the ear. (Follow the instructions for Make the Eyes on the next page.) Or not. Turn the ear right side out.

7 Repeat steps 4, 5, and 6 to make the second ear. Set the ears aside.

Make the Head

1 Align the face (C) and the outer crown (B) along the crown's short edge and the face's long edge, right sides together. Pin them in place.

Pink Nauseator

Blue Nauseator

2 Backstitch them together, leaving a ¼-inch (6 mm) seam allowance.

3 Place the horns (G) or ears (H) atop the outer crown, between ½ and 1 inch (1.3 and 2.5 cm) back from where the face and outer crown come together. Make sure the horns or ears are pointing toward the face, right sides touching right sides. Align the open edges of the appendages with the edge of the outer crown. Don't pin the horns or ears in place—you won't be able to see the pin when you sew the seam and you might poke yourself with it.

4 Lining up the side panels (A) is a little bit tricky. Align one faux-fur side panel with the long edge of the crown, right sides together. Make sure the front of the side panel touches the face of the Nauseator. (Look at the label on pattern A to see where the face should attach.) Pin the pieces together. Backstitch along the edge, leaving a ⅜-inch (9.5 mm) seam allowance.

5 Repeat step 4 to attach the other side panel.

6 To make the inside of the Nauseator, repeat steps 3, 4, and 5 using the crown lining pattern (D) and the fleece or cotton inner side panels (A). Do not use the face pattern again.

7 If you like, cut a piece of hook-and-loop tape that fits inside the ends of the flaps. Make sure you have a piece of the hook side and the loop side of the tape. Backstitch one side of the hook-and-loop tape on the right side of the first fleece or cotton flap. Backstitch the other side to the opposite flap.

Do you want your Nauseator to have slatted eyelids or half-open eyelids?

Make the Eyes

1 If you want your Nauseator to have slatted eyelids, like the ones on Blue Nauseator in the photo, first pin the eyelids (F) to the face. The wrong side of the eyelids should touch the right side of the face. Backstitch them in place, leaving a ⅜-inch (9.5 mm) seam allowance. Carefully cut the eyelid open between the seams. (Don't cut the seams!)

2 If you want the half-open eyelids, like the ones on Pink Nauseator, cut the eyelid pieces in half before sewing them onto the face. See the optional cut line on the eyelid template.

3 Place the half-eyelids right side up. Attach them to the face by sewing around the top, curved outer edge only, leaving a ⅜-inch (9.5 mm) seam allowance.

4 Use the fabric pen to make a mark on the wrong side of the face. Center this mark inside the half-eyelid seam (feel for it with your hands). Repeat behind the other eyelid.

5 On each mark, snip a small hole no wider than the shaft of the doll eye.

6 Insert a child-safe doll eye into the hole, sliding it under the eyelid flap or flaps so that the shaft pokes through to the wrong side of the creature. Secure the washer on the shaft. Repeat to attach the other eye.

Put Your Heads Together

1 Place the teeth atop the face so the right side of the teeth touch the right side of the face. Match the straight edges of the teeth with the bottom edge of the face.

2 Flip the interior head wrong side out. Keep the exterior head right side out. Align the interior and exterior heads, right sides together. Match the edges and flaps and pin the pieces together. Make sure to put a pin through each tooth to hold it in place.

3 Now you're ready to sew the heads together. Starting at the back, backstitch around the edge of one flap and back up, across the bottom of the face, down the second flap, and back up. Leave the back edge open.

4 Turn the Nauseator right side out, lining inside, and sew the opening closed. If you haven't done so already, now is the time to remove all of the pins.

Wear your Nauseator Helmet with all of the pride you can muster. Expect to turn heads and frighten young and old people alike. And a few dogs and cats.

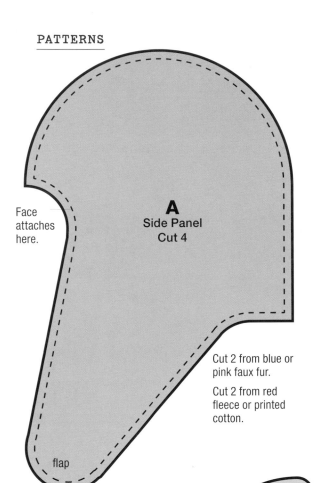

A
Side Panel
Cut 4

Face attaches here.

flap

Cut 2 from blue or pink faux fur.

Cut 2 from red fleece or printed cotton.

Nauseator
enlarge 250%

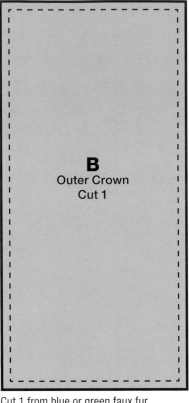

B
Outer Crown
Cut 1

Cut 1 from blue or green faux fur.

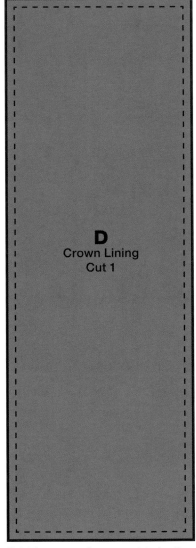

D
Crown Lining
Cut 1

Cut 1 from green fleece or printed cotton.

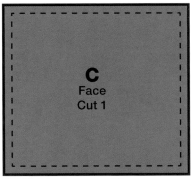

C
Face
Cut 1

Cut 1 from orange or red fleece.

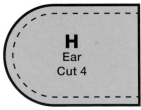

H
Ear
Cut 4

Cut 2 from blue faux fur.
Cut 2 from red fleece.

G
Horn
Cut 4

Cut 4 from yellow fleece.

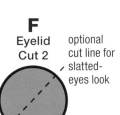

F
Eyelid
Cut 2

optional cut line for slatted-eyes look

Cut 2 from orange or red fleece.

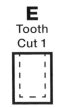

E
Tooth
Cut 1

Cut 1 from white felt.

Beast of Burden Emerges from Whirlpool

Coastal dwellers report hearing the chant "I'll carry that for you!"

You Will Need

- Patterns (page 93)
- Basic Beastie Kit (page 8)
- Orange felt, 1 yard (91.4 cm)
- Gold felt, 1 yard (91.4 cm)
- Purple felt, 1 yard (91.4 cm)
- Light green felt, 8 x 8 inches (20.3 x 20.3 cm)
- Polyester thread in gold
- Upholstery thread in whatever color you like
- 2 child-safe doll eyes (or as many as you like)

A sewing machine is recommended for this project because of the length of the seams.

Use the fabrics and colors noted on the patterns and the supplies list, or use whatever fabrics you like.

Making and Using Templates

1. Use the patterns to create templates. Trace and cut your pieces from the fabrics. (If you're using a fabric other than felt, always cut from the wrong side.) For the arm (C) piece, see step 2. Set all the pieces aside.

2. Measure the distance between your hip and your shoulder opposite that hip. Add 12 inches (30.5 cm) to that measurement. The resulting number is the length you'll use for the arm pieces. The width will be 4½ inches (21.6 cm).

3. Create a rectangular template with those dimensions and use it to cut out four arm pieces from the orange felt. Set the pieces aside.

This beast is big. Make some room for piecing it together.

Constructing the Body

1. Grab the body (A) pieces. Align their edges. (If using a fabric other than felt, place the pieces right sides together.) Secure the matched edges with pins.

2. Leaving a ¼-inch (6 mm) seam allowance, backstitch the body pieces together at their matched edges. Leave one of the short edges open. Set it aside.

3. Grab the tongue (B) pieces. Align their edges. (If using a fabric other than felt, place the pieces right sides together.) Secure the matched edges with pins.

4. Leaving a ¼-inch (6 mm) seam allowance, backstitch the tongue pieces together at their matched edges. Leave the straight edge open. Turn the tongue right side out.

5. Insert the tongue, right side out, into the open edge of the assembled body, which is still wrong side out. Align the edges, matching the seams at the edges of the tongue to the seams at the edges of the body. (See diagram 1.)

6. Leaving a ¼-inch (6 mm) seam allowance, backstitch the aligned edges. Leave 4 inches (10.2 cm) unstitched so you can turn these assembled items right side out. (See diagram 2.) Carefully turn the tongue and body right side out. Use the unstitched portion as an opening to lightly and evenly stuff the tongue. Do not stuff the body.

7. Turn the edges of the stuffing hole inward, and use a whipstitch to close it. Be careful not to let any of the stuffing slip from the tongue into the body.

8. To close off the tongue from the body, carefully backstitch the seam where they connect. Make sure your needle goes in through the seam on one side, and out through the seam on the other side each time. (See diagram 3.) Depending on your skill this could take ages, so pop in a video or set the phone to speaker and call a relative.

9 Once the tongue and the body are closed off from one another, run a backstitch down the middle of the tongue, perpendicular to the connecting seam (over which you've just agonized with a relative on the phone) all the way to the tip. As you do this, make sure the stuffing remains evenly distributed. Incidentally, you may wish to phone another relative to help pass the time.

Whew. That was some work. Take it easy as you create the arms for this creature.

Constructing the Arms

1 Grab the arm (C) pieces. Align two pieces to create an arm. (If using a fabric other than felt, place the pieces right sides together.) Secure the matched edges with pins.

2 Leaving a ¼-inch (6 mm) seam allowance, backstitch around the edges. Leave a 2-inch (5 cm) stuffing hole about halfway up the arm. Also leave one short edge open. (The arms are so long that it will be easier to stuff them if you have two holes.) Repeat for the second pair of arm pieces.

3 Remove the pins. Carefully turn each arm right side out. Stuff the arms as firmly as you like. Whipstitch to close the stuffing holes on the sides of the arm. Do not close the remaining open ends of the arms. Set both arms aside.

Making the Face

1 Grab the face (D) pieces. Align their edges. (If using a fabric other than felt, place the pieces right sides together.) Secure the matched edges with pins.

2 Leaving a ¼-inch (6 mm) seam allowance, use the yellow thread to backstitch the face pieces together at their matched edges. Leave one of the short edges open.

3 Remove the pins. Gently turn the face right side out.

4 It's time to put the eyes on. Use your fabric pen to make two marks on the face about 2½ inches (6.4 cm) above its open edge.

5 On each mark, snip a small hole no wider than the shaft of the eye you'll insert there.

6 Insert the shaft of one of the eyes into an eyehole. The shaft should extend into the wrong side of the face. Secure the washer on the shaft. Repeat this step for the other eyehole.

7 Lightly stuff the face. Set aside.

8 Grab the teeth (E) pieces. Align their edges. (If using a fabric other than felt, place the pieces right sides together.) Secure the matched edges with pins.

9 Leaving a ¼-inch (6 mm) seam allowance, backstitch the teeth pieces together. Leave the straight edges open.

Face Sandwiching Time

1 Remove the pins. Carefully turn the teeth right side out. Lightly stuff the teeth. Set aside.

2 Fold the face, short end to short end, matching the open edge to the closed edge. Insert the teeth between these two edges so that they're sandwiched between the folded layers of the face. Align the open edge of the teeth with the edges of the face. The eyes and teeth will be on the inside of the fold. Pin the pieces together along the edges.

3 Leaving a ¼-inch (6 mm) seam allowance, backstitch the pieces together. The face should be in the shape of a tube.

4 Gently turn the assembled face right side out so the eyes and teeth are on the outside.

Have you noticed the Beast just staring at you with those eyes? Maybe it's thinking, "Hurry up and finish me."

Assembling this Creature

(1) Grab your stuffed arms and butt the open ends together. Use upholstery thread to join the arms by tightly whipstitching the open edges together, creating a single tube. Repeat this step to reinforce the seam. (See diagram 4.)

(2) Slide the face tube up one side of the strap arms until it covers the arms' seam. There's no need to stitch it into place. It won't move when you are using it as a shoulder pad.

Attach the Arms to the Body

(1) Return to the body and tongue combination. Find the horizontal point halfway between the body's bottom edge and the seam where it attaches to the tongue.

(2) Place the ends of the arms at either side of this mid-point and pin them there. (See diagram 5.)

(3) With the body's midpoint pinned to the arms, fold the body upward, aligning its long edges with the arms. Pin the body to the arms where they meet. (See diagram 6.)

(4) Use upholstery thread to make a tight whipstitch on the interior side of the bag to secure the body to the arms. Start at the seam where the tongue meets the body. Continue whipstitching down the arm, around its end at the body's midpoint, and back up to the end of the body. (See diagram 7.) Attach both arms this way. Reinforce these seams with further whipstitching as much as you can. This is an important, load-bearing attachment.

When you've attached the arms, flop the tongue through the arms and over your new bag's opening. You've likely guessed by now that the tongue is the bag's closure.

This beast is meant for a light burden. Use it to carry all the projects you've made in this book, or your day planner and travel coffee mug.

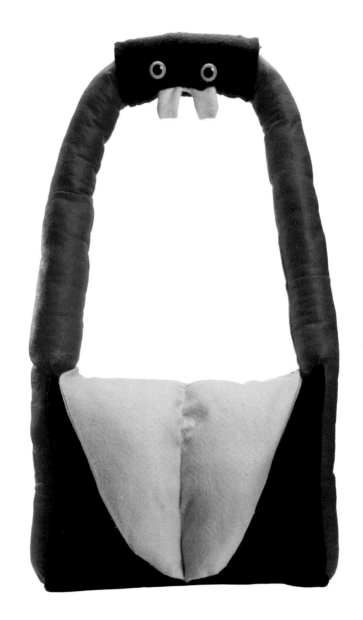

PATTERNS

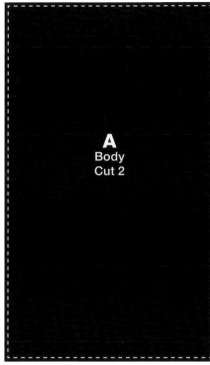

A
Body
Cut 2

Cut 2 from purple felt.

Create a template 26 inches (66 cm) long and 16 inches (40.6 cm) wide.

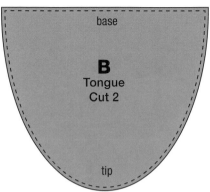

base

B
Tongue
Cut 2

tip

Cut 2 from yellow felt.

Create a template 12½ inches (31.8 cm) long, 12½ inches (31.8 cm) wide at the base, and 3 inches (7.6 cm) wide at the tip.

C
Arm
Cut 4

Cut 4 from orange felt.

You must determine the length for the arm pattern so that the messenger bag is the right size for you. See the instructions.

E
Teeth
Cut 2

Cut 2 from lime felt.

Create a template 1½ inches (3.8 cm) long and 2½ inches (6.4 cm) wide. Each tooth is 1¼ inches (3.2 cm) wide.

D
Face
Cut 2

Cut 2 from purple felt.

Create a template 9½ inches (24.1 cm) long and 8½ inches (21.6 cm) wide.

DIAGRAMS

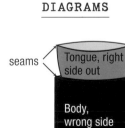

seams — Tongue, right side out — seams

Body, wrong side out

1.

Tongue, right sides together

Body, wrong side out

2.

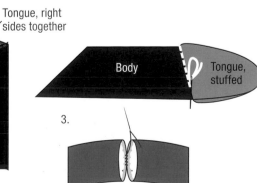

Body — Tongue, stuffed

3.

4.

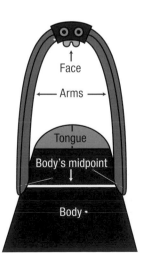

Face

Arms

Tongue

Body's midpoint

Body

5.

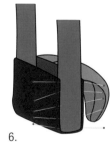

6.

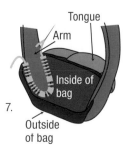

Tongue
Arm
Inside of bag
Outside of bag

7.

Glossary

Anchoring. The technique of securing thread in fabric by tying a knot at the long end of the thread. This knot keeps the thread from pulling through the fabric when you sew.

Appendage. A big word for most any part that projects from the main body.

Appliqué. To apply one layer of fabric over another to create a design or pattern.

Assembly. Sewing pieces together.

Backstitch. One of the most commonly used hand-sewing methods for creating a seam. Instructions on page 12.

Batting. Bulky fabric or fiber material used for stuffing.

Button. Flat piece of plastic or other material used on clothing to hold parts together.

Child-safe cat eyes. Eyes with slanted pupils that attach securely to your creature so that they won't come off and choke children.

Child-safe doll eyes. Eyes with round pupils that attach securely to your creature so that they won't come off and choke children.

Cotton. Fabric woven or knitted from cotton fiber. It's typically thin and lightweight.

Craft scissors. Tool to cut paper, card stock, and thread.

Cut lines. The solid lines on the outside edges of each pattern that show you where to cut.

Diagram. A simple drawing showing the basic layout of a project.

Fabric. Cloth of any type.

Fabric pen. A special type of marker designed to write on fabric without bleeding.

Fabric scissors. Scissors used only for cutting cloth.

Faux fur. Shaggy polyester that looks like an animal's coat (except that it might be bright red or electric blue).

Felt. Fabric made from wool or synthetic materials. It's typically sturdy and can be thick or thin.

Felted. Wool that's been matted to make it thick and fuzzy.

Fleece. Soft fabric with a brushed or woolly texture.

Googly eyes. Fake eyes with pupils that move.

Hem. A neat edge on cloth made by folding the fabric over and stitching it down.

Hot glue. A hot, melted adhesive applied with an electric, gun-shaped tool.

Hot-glue gun. A tool that contains a heating element that melts and applies hot-glue sticks.

Instructions. Directions for how to do or make something.

Lining. A layer of material used to cover an inside surface.

Needle. A thin metal sewing tool with a point at one end for puncturing fabric and a hole at the other that a thread is passed through.

Notch. A little slit cut in the edge of the fabric near the seam along a curve. Notches keep sewn fabric from bunching. Notching is the act of creating a notch.

Pattern. A guide or model for making something.

Pile. The direction the strands of faux fur "grows."

Pin. A thin piece of metal with a blunt head and sharp tip that can pierce fabric. Or, the action of holding fabric together with pins where corners meet and where you intend to sew a seam.

Polyester. Fabric made from synthetic fibers. It can be thick and tufted like hair or thin and smooth like silk fabric.

Right sides together. Laying fabric with the prettiest or fuzziest sides facing each other.

Sandwich. To put between. In these projects, you will often sandwich appendages between the two (facing) right sides of the fabric.

Seam. Where you sew two pieces of fabric together.

Seam allowance. The distance you leave between the seam you will sew and the edge of the fabric, so that the fabric won't unravel.

Seam allowance lines. Dotted lines inside the cut line on each pattern. See also seam allowance.

Sewing. Using a needle and thread to join pieces of fabric.

Stitch. A length of thread that has been passed through one or more pieces of fabric to join them or create decoration. Also, a specific type of sewing. See also backstitch, straight stitch, whipstitch, and zigzag stitch.

Straight pins. See pin.

Straight stitch. A hand-sewing technique that draws a single thread in a straight line through the front side of the fabric being sewn. Instructions on page 13.

Stuffing. What you use to fill a plush monster.

Template. A guide for cutting fabric pieces. It's usually made of card stock or another sturdy, flat material and is laid atop the wrong side of the fabric to be cut. A template is made from a pattern.

Thread. A fine cord of twisted fibers. Also, to pass one end of a thread through the eye of a needle. This is the first step to sewing.

Turning tool. Specialized craft tool with a rounded point that you can stick into corner seams to turn out ears and other odd shapes.

Tying off. Securing the thread in place when you finish sewing by knotting it in a special way after the last stitch.

Unravel. When the threads of fabric separate and come undone.

Upholstery. Related to cushions for chairs and couches.

Whipstitch. A hand-sewing technique used to bind edges, to prevent unraveling. Instructions on page 13.

Zigzag stitch. A stitch in a pattern of Ms or Ws usually done on a sewing machine. It's usually used for attaching facial features and binding edges so they don't unravel. Instructions on page 15.

Designer Credits

Ian Dennis: Beast of Burden (page 89), Totebaggers (page 58), Xipp It (page 50), Pocket Mouth (page 33), and Tri-Plod (page 30). Ian crafts the Slow Children (Playing) line of toys, available at stupidcreatures.com.

Jenny Harada: Feeteaters (page 80), Floppyzoid (page 54), the Aliens and Spaceship (page 44), and Big Belly (page 40). Her work appears in books and galleries, and at craft fairs. www.jennyharada.com

John Murphy: Nauseators (page 84), Pursivals (page 74), Thingtones (page 68), Creepers of the Door (page 62), Cosmic Three (page 36), and Juju Triplets (page 22). He's the author of *Stupid Sock Creatures*. See more at www.stupidcreatures.com.

Index